The Encyclicals of John Paul II:
Foundations of Catholic Faith
and Morality

To Rev. Raphal
Zwolenkiewicz

with warm regards.

Fr. Zbigniew Tybarski
March 9, 2012

The Encyclicals of John Paul II: Foundations of Catholic Faith and Morality

Fr. Zbigniew Tyburski

Sapientia Press
of Ave Maria University

Imprimi Potest: Sister Kathleen Flanagan, S.C., Ph.D.

Imprimatur: ✝ Bishop Arthur J. Serratelli, S.T.D., S.S.L., D.D.
Bishop of Paterson
August 9, 2010

Requests for permission to make copies of any part of the work should be directed to:

Sapientia Press
of Ave Maria University
5050 Ave Maria Blvd.
Ave Maria, FL 34142
888-343-8607

Cover design: Eloise Anagnost

Cover photo: © LOCHON FRANCOIS/GAMMA

Printed in the United States of America.

Library of Congress Control Number: 2011940177

ISBN 978-1-932589-60-3

To my dear parents, Józefa and Bolesław,
in gratitude for humility and rectitude of life.

—Zbigniew

Contents

Acknowledgments

FIRST OF ALL, I express gratitude to my dear friend Jan Haszek, with whom I discussed the idea of this publication, as well as each step of its writing. I want to indicate special thanks to the Sisters of Saints Cyril and Methodius in Danville, Pennsylvania, where I was privileged, through the mediation of Helen Figiel, to have spent my vacation in 2009; there I found quiet inspiration for developing part of this document close to the chapel of Eucharistic perpetual adoration. I would also like to express my gratitude to Mr. Lawrence Daly and Mr. Eugene Biancheri, who provided constructive criticism and helpful suggestions during the preparation of this manuscript.

Of course, the deepest debt of gratitude is to the spirit of John Paul II, to whom I often pray, and to God, who allowed me to prepare this book and select the best phrases to represent the most important ideas written by the Pope in his encyclicals.

Foreword

THE LONG PONTIFICATE of Pope John Paul II (1978–2005) is one of considerable importance for the history of the Catholic Church. As the first non-Italian pope in more than four centuries, and the first-ever pope from Eastern Europe, Pope John Paul II presided over the collapse of the Communist empire, refashioned the papal office, energized a new generation of Catholics, especially young "John Paul II" priests, and brought the Petrine Office to almost every corner of the globe. The iconic images of this Pope—conscious of the world stage upon which he was placed—are too numerous to list in full, but include the Papal Mass in downtown Warsaw, the opening of the Holy Door in 2000, the visit to the Central Synagogue of Rome, the visit to his would-be assassin in prison, World Youth Days, and even his funeral in Saint Peter's Square, among many others. As a participant myself in the media coverage of the papal transition in 2005, I was fascinated to witness firsthand the individual and corporate impact of this Pope on the media community alone. Virtually every reporter and commentator had a story of their own personal experience of Pope John Paul the Great.

As a philosopher, theologian, and writer of considerable depth and skill, Pope John Paul II had the inclination, as well as the opportunity presented by a long pontificate, to craft a carefully worded spiritual legacy in the fourteen encyclicals of his papacy. These run the gamut from those issued to commemorate specific historic moments in the life of the Church (*Slavorum Apostoli* and *Centesimus Annus*), to those which treat of the human vocation (*Sollicitudo Rei Socialis* and *Evangelium Vitae*), to those which soar into the very mystery of the Godhead (*Redemptor Hominis* and *Dominum et Vivificantem*).

Some, like *Dives in Misericordia*, are intensely theological. Others are groundbreaking, such as *Redemptor Hominis*, the first papal encyclical on Christian anthropology; *Dominum et Vivificantem*, the most comprehensive papal teaching ever on the work of the Holy Spirit; and *Ut Unum Sint*, in which the Supreme Pontiff asks his fellow Christians for forgiveness and invites them to propose new models for the Petrine Office. From the more than twenty-six years of his pontificate, there are thousands of documents bearing Pope John Paul's name and authority, including apostolic constitutions, apostolic letters, apostolic exhortations, and homilies. But the fourteen encyclicals, addressed to the whole Church, and in some cases to all of mankind, constitute a unique and very personal gift to the Church, and a repository of the Pope's own spirituality and theological reflection. It is known that part of the rare papal "time off" was actually time fully committed to the research, reflection, writing, and revision necessary for the production of these encyclicals.[1]

Because these encyclicals are so central to the mind and soul of this great Pope, Fr. Tyburski's book makes a significant contribution to the English-speaking world by providing an insightful, balanced, and succinct synopsis of the content of each of these encyclicals. This is especially important because of the length and theological complexity of the encyclicals themselves. Here is presented not only the opportunity to grasp the main themes and ideas of each encyclical, but also the chance to compare them to one another and see the development of some themes across the broad spectrum of John Paul II's entire encyclical *corpus*. For example, papal biographer George Weigel notes in his own speeches and writing the seven distinct "souls" of Pope John Paul II.[2] In Fr. Tyburski's volume, one is able to trace the influence and development of the Pontiff's "Marian" soul and "apostolic" soul across the breadth of several encyclicals. This work gives us the opportunity to find similarities and contrasts within the entire corpus of John Paul II's encyclical writing and appreciate the broad themes and message that connect them together and form a distinct spiritual treasure.

In addition to being able to appreciate each individual encyclical within the larger framework of Pope John Paul II's writing, Fr. Tyburski's book

---

[1] George Weigel, *Witness to Hope* (New York: Harper Collins, 1999), 419, 558.

[2] Weigel enumerates the Polish, Carmelite, Marian, apostolic, lay, humanistic, and dramatic "souls" of Pope John Paul II. George Weigel, lecture at Seton Hall University, October 4, 2000.

also offers the reader two other important perspectives. First, it provides the "back story" of each encyclical. We become aware of the issues that prompted the writing of each particular encyclical. In addition to the historical and theological issues, we are also made privy to issues from Pope John Paul's own life experience, his Polish background, his pastoral experience, and his experience of the Second Vatican Council, which find their way into the encyclical. In a sense, the author invites us into the mind and experience of the Holy Father, and we have the opportunity to see not only how the Pontiff's different experiences come together in the encyclical, but even how Pope John Paul himself grows in his understanding as he fashions the document.

Secondly, we also have the opportunity to appreciate the spiritual, liturgical, historical, Marian, and contemporary roots of the encyclicals. We are invited to understand them not only in the context of the other encyclicals, but also in their relationship to other papal writings, and encyclicals of previous papacies.

In his masterful biography of Pope John Paul II, George Weigel describes the particular pastoral approach of the Pope, developed in his early days as a university chaplain. In Polish, the word is *Srodowisko*, a word not easily translated into English, but perhaps best rendered as "accompaniment."[3] Those who were attracted to the young Fr. Karol Wojtyla or, later, to Pope John Paul II, found in him a spiritual companion accompanying them in their journey of faith. In his volume on the John Paul II encyclicals, Fr. Tyburski has not merely opened up the complexity of the encyclicals themselves, but has opened up papal *Srodowisko* to the reader, allowing the late Holy Father to continue to accompany us today on our own spiritual journeys.

I have been happy to have the opportunity to read Fr. Tyburski's work, and have been enlightened by it in so many ways. I am happy to recommend it, not only as a reference work for any serious student of the modern papacy, but also to all who wish to deepen their faith under the guidance of Pope John Paul II.

—*Rev. Msgr. Raymond J. Kupke*
June 24, 2010

---

[3] Weigel, *Witness to Hope*, 98–102.

Preface

POPE JOHN PAUL II was truly a man for everyone. In all corners of the globe, people greeted him with great enthusiasm. They felt he opened his arms and his heart to them. He often broke the Vatican's security rules and entered into a crowd—taking children into his arms, greeting the sick, touching thousands of people, shaking their hands. In addition to his many pilgrimages, the Pope met with leaders, politicians, and diplomats of different nations and cultures. For over twenty-six years of his pontificate, John Paul II discussed religious topics about God, as well as the fate of humanity, in his homilies and speeches. He also addressed these subjects in his letters, decrees, and encyclicals.

An encyclical is an official document issued by a pope that is addressed to the bishops and the faithful of the whole Church on matters of great importance related to Christian life, with the purpose of maintaining unity of faith. Some of the encyclicals are directed to all people of good will, while others, such as *Veritatis Splendor*, to Catholic bishops alone.

The main message that permeates most of John Paul's encyclicals is his desire to renew Catholic faith and morality and to protect Catholics against any deviation or degradation. He also wanted to rescue the modern world from the brink of moral disaster. The incredible and often confusing quantity of information available, mainly caused by the digital revolution, may soon render many people incapable of distinguishing good from evil.

Although many publications have attempted to bring the messages contained in the papal encyclicals closer to the general public, their deep content is not yet widely known. The reasons for this are the length of the encyclicals themselves (each is from 60 to 110 pages) and the author's often difficult theological and philosophical language.

I have had a lifelong interest in all the papal social encyclicals, and Pope John Paul II wrote three of this kind. My original intent was to prepare a short article on these three, but later decided to write a book summarizing all fourteen encyclicals, for the spiritual benefit of all readers.

The messages of the encyclicals, each in a condensed form and expressed in simpler language, should inspire readers to reflect on their faith and its moral implications and on the fundamental convictions regarding the nature of God, world, and humanity, as the book's title indicates. I hope also that many will find liberating truth here in the pages of these commentaries. John Paul II wrote in his eighth encyclical, *Redemptoris Missio*, quoting the Second Vatican Council Declaration on Religious Freedom, *Dignitatis Humanae*, that all people are "bound to hold to the truth once it is known, and to regulate their whole lives by its demands."

Shortly after the text of my work was completed and provided to the publishing house, the Vatican announced that on May 1, 2011 a ceremony of beatification for John Paul II would take place in Rome. Beatification is an important step preceding the declaration of sainthood. Many people are waiting for this step; not just Catholics. The Holy Father was admired and loved by followers of many different religions; even by unbelievers standing far from God and the Catholic Church. This event may help to diminish mental anguish and hostility, as well as bring people together, especially those who have been divided by hate, violence, injustice, and war. The modern world is headed toward the unknown with rapid rate of changes in social life, fragile economies, new technologies, and rejection of higher values. Blessed John Paul II will be an excellent role model—especially for young people—for how to live in this world, realize one's personal vocation, and fulfill God's will in heaven. A familiarity with the Pope's biography inspires us to live according to God's Commandments, with love for each human being. To more fully follow his example, it is necessary to understand Pope John Paul II's teachings, especially those written in his encyclicals.

—*Fr. Zbigniew Tyburski*

1

The Redeemer of Man
(*Redemptor Hominis*)

March 4, 1979

Introduction

JESUS CHRIST the Redeemer overcomes human evil and bestows his divine love on humanity. He confers a new dignity of being a child of God on every person and illumines the splendor of his divine truth into the darkness of our minds and hearts. In every generation, he calls those who are to be signs of his presence in our midst in order to make the fruits of his saving Passion and glorious Resurrection available to everyone. Pope John Paul II was such a sign for the world toward the end of the second millennium.

The Pope was fully aware of his enormous responsibility, and his untiring efforts to make everyone know the love of God as revealed to us in Jesus Christ bear witness to it. John Paul covered countless miles on all inhabited continents to proclaim personally the Good News of salvation. Where he could not go in person, he would send his emissaries, and to everyone he wrote fourteen encyclical letters to express his concerns for the comprehensive welfare of humanity.

In his first encyclical, *Redemptor Hominis* (*The Redeemer of Man*), Pope John Paul II teaches that Jesus Christ is the center of the universe. Humanity is next in closeness to this center. Jesus the Son of God became human—like us in everything except sin. Yet he was not indifferent to the sinfulness of humanity. While on earth, Jesus recognized sin all around him and conquered it with his love. Jesus still knows that man is unhappy when living in sin. Man is primarily created to live in happiness with Jesus in the center of the universe, our pure consciousness being ultimately united with him, the fruit of divine love.

God created the first man with all the love of his heart, and even the sin of Adam did not extinguish the flame of this divine benevolence. The expulsion from Paradise was a natural consequence of Adam's transgression, but God's response, the promise of a Redeemer, appears as the greatest proof of his steadfast love for humanity. When centuries later the Son of God was born among us, the promise was fulfilled. Jesus, the Divine Redeemer, saved us though his death and Resurrection and invited us to participate in God's life both here on earth and in heaven after our death.

We are invited to share in God's life as individuals united in the community of the Church. John Paul II, following the lead of the Second Vatican Council, defines the Church as the "People of God." When writing about mankind as a whole, that is, about the People of God in the broad sense of the term, John Paul underlines the need for the correct exercise of the faculty of freedom. He teaches that we can become slaves to our own weaknesses as a result of the incorrect use of the gift of freedom. In this way, we can degrade our own humanity. In response, the Church reaches out toward all and points to the Good News of Jesus. The whole mission of the Church focuses on service to mankind and leading it to salvation. This activity justifies Pope John Paul II's description of man as "the way of the Church." Therefore, the Church aids all who will listen, to understand the teaching of Jesus. Thanks to the mediation of the Church, everyone can participate in God's plan of salvation fulfilled in Christ, the Redeemer of Man.

John Paul discusses other important themes in *Redemptor Hominis*, such as the collegial nature of the Church, human rights, and human vocations among many others. Beginning with his reflection on the Redeemer of Man, the Pope outlines the program for his whole pontificate.

Jesus Christ—The Redeemer of Man

We often hear, either at home or during religious instruction, about the infidelity of Adam toward God. We learn from the descriptive biblical narrative about the fall of the first couple that Adam freely chose to eat from the tree in the middle of Paradise despite God's command to the contrary. This disobedience, called original sin, made all of humanity incapable of reciprocating God's friendship. People were not in the position to redress their pitiful situation after the sin of Adam. God, on his part, did not leave humanity in despair and promised a Redeemer who would restore the shattered relationship between himself and us. People awaited the fulfillment of this promise for centuries, while prophets periodically announced that the Redeemer would come.

In *Redemptor Hominis*, John Paul II makes us aware that redemption is the work of God's love in the life of every person. His contention is based on the New Testament statement of John 3:16: "For God so loved the world that he gave his only Son, so that everyone who believes in him might not perish but might have eternal life." The Pope's argument is also supported by Saint Paul's description of the restoration in Christ of the link between God and man that was broken in Adam (see Rom 5:12–21). We can therefore easily understand that thanks to the Redeemer, humanity "recovers again its original link with the divine source of Wisdom and Love" (*RH* 8).

Humanity redeemed in Christ finds a new sense of life on earth and gains the prospect of eternal life. It obtains, as John Paul II teaches, full awareness of its dignity and elevation. Jesus' act of redemption has a divine dimension as well. The Pope tells us that Jesus Christ "satisfied the Father's eternal love . . . which man in a way rejected" (*RH* 9). Additionally, in the Cross of Jesus, God found a chance to reveal himself to us as the God of redemption, and not only as the Creator. In Jesus' death and Resurrection, God found the best possible way of telling us that love is greater than sin and death, because "God is love" (1 Jn 4:8, 16).

A very prominent aspect of the Pope's teaching is the explicit inclusion of every person in the work of redemption. Consequently, there is hope of participating in the life of Christ the Redeemer for everyone, not only those who are strong in their faith, but also those who are weak in one way or another. What ultimately counts is the decision to rectify one's life and to allow God to embrace us with his love. We cannot exclude anyone, since redemption in Christ is open to all humanity.

Collegiality of the Church

John Paul II, as Peter's successor, is the visible head of the Church, but he is acutely aware that he cannot proclaim the message of Christ alone. The Pope wants his service to be carried out in communion with the whole Church, and the principle of collegiality expresses and ensures the unity of the Church in a very powerful way. This is the reason why the Pope reflects on this principle at the very beginning of his encyclical—and, we may say, at the very beginning of his pontificate (*RH* 5).

The word *collegiality* derives from the Latin *collegium*, which means "assembly" or "gathering." The first assembly of this type was formed by Jesus himself when he called the twelve apostles and placed Peter as the head of this group (see Mt 10:1–4 and 16:17–19). Jesus is thus the One who introduced the principle of collegiality into his Church, and we can see it at work in the Acts of the Apostles, most especially perhaps during the so-called Jerusalem Council (see Acts 15). The principle was expressed in many different forms throughout the history of the Church, while the current structure was elaborated during the Second Vatican Council (initiated by Pope John XXIII in 1962 and concluded by Pope Paul VI in 1965). Among other things, Paul VI founded the Synod of Bishops as a permanent organ of collegiality, as requested by the Council. John Paul II expresses his satisfaction with the way the Synod has served the Church ever since it was established. We must remember that the ecumenical council itself is the most solemn expression of the principle of collegiality.

We should bear in mind that the collegiality of the Church functions differently than democracy in a modern society. Collegiality of the Church stems from its original mission. Jesus chose twelve apostles and entrusted them with this mission: to bring everyone to the Church and to bring the Church to everyone. Similarly, the Pope confirms every bishop in the Church, whom he subsequently sends to his diocese (mission). A bishop in turn, entrusts every priest in the diocese with work to do. Bishops' regular visits to the pope (called *ad limina Apostolorum* in Latin) are the principal means of expressing episcopal collegiality. These visits serve, among other things, to express the bishops' unity with the pope, to provide an account of the state of their dioceses, and to give them a chance to honor the tombs of Saints Peter and Paul. When discussing the collegiality of the Church, we should not forget that the Church has both human and divine dimensions. Even though she comprises earthly structures (the Vatican, cathedrals, and churches), her head is Christ, living in the holy sacraments, while the deposit of divine truth is guarded in the Church by the Holy Spirit.

Synods of the universal Church, as well as those at a local level (diocesan), are organized according to the guidance of the Second Vatican

Council and in accordance with teachings of the popes. The task of these assemblies is to care for the faithful in matters related to faith and morals. Councils of priests, synods, and pastoral councils are set up in each diocese. Similar situations occur within parishes. Pastoral, ecumenical, and evangelizing councils are formed with the participation of both priests and laity. By means of this collegial service, the Church seeks to help each individual find his way to God. The Church's mission is to lead people to salvation and to the experience of God's love.

Humanity in God's Plans

Having placed his encyclical in its immediate context of the Catholic Church (see preceding section on collegiality), John Paul II begins the analysis of the mystery of redemption itself. As the Shepherd of Christ's flock after the example of Peter, the Pope turns to Jesus Christ whom he calls "the good Shepherd of all men" (*RH* 13). He describes in his document the situation of modern humanity with the words of Peter, which the apostle addressed to Jesus: "Master, to whom shall we go? You have the words of eternal life" (Jn 6:68). The Pope teaches that we can only find better understanding of ourselves and meaning in our lives if we follow the one who is "the way and the truth and the life" (Jn 14:6). Quoting the Scriptures, John Paul stresses that only in God can we find "all the treasures of wisdom and knowledge" (Col 2:3).

The Pope makes us aware that not every person is able to recognize the divinity of Christ. Remember, it even had to be revealed to Peter before he could say, "You are the Messiah, the Son of the living God" (Mt 16:16). Many, instead, are first attracted by the humanity of Jesus and the noble characteristics of his life. For many contemporary people, the most precious values that Jesus represents are "his fidelity to the truth, his all-embracing love" (*RH* 7).

John Paul II teaches us that because of Jesus' Incarnation and life on earth, he has experienced all aspects of our human existence except sin (see Heb 4:15 and *RH* 8). He took this humanity of ours to the Cross, overcame our sin by his death, and opened for us the way to new life by his Resurrection. We can thus say that Jesus Christ has restored in us the original design of God and revealed our status as God's children. Moreover, only he enables us to understand ourselves fully when we approach him in the depths of our hearts. The Pope tells us that we can grasp the whole grandeur of our being only when we are united with Christ (*RH* 10).

Approaching Christ not only helps us understand who we are, but it also makes us even more complete. We change in the process of knowing ourselves in Christ. We are created anew as we make the fruits of redemption our own. We are "newly created," as the Pope puts it (*RH* 10). An analogy with quantum physics comes to mind, where the very act of observing changes the state of the object observed. But even the Pope can only quote Saint Paul to express the fruits of this change taking place in us during the process of self-discovery in Christ: "There is neither Jew nor Greek, there is neither slave nor free, there is neither male nor female; for you are all one in Christ Jesus" (Gal 3:28, in *RH* 10).

Complete communion in Christ the Redeemer is thus revealed as the amazing and marvelous destiny of every human being in God's plan. We are invited to take an active part in the process of realizing this plan, but this is the topic of the next section—that on human freedom.

Human Freedom

Often people today do not fully understand the concept of freedom and are convinced that they are free only when they use this gift in an arbitrary fashion. John Paul II teaches in his encyclical that the source of true freedom is the recognition of the truth about oneself, in other words, self-knowledge. The best way to arrive at this kind of knowledge is by forging a personal relationship with Christ, who called himself "the way and the truth and the life" (Jn 14:6). After all, he came to earth to make all people free and to liberate us all from moral evil. This is what internal freedom really means. Jesus' words in the Gospel of John are particularly telling in this regard: "You will know the truth, and the truth will set you free" (Jn 8:32). Let us remember that it is only a freedom based on truth that saves us from all that can limit or reduce this freedom. Those who reject God and his truth in the name of falsely understood freedom usually end up imprisoned within themselves, thus bringing about suffering on themselves and others. In his attempt to protect us from this kind of suffering, the Pope urges us "to avoid every kind of illusory freedom, every superficial unilateral freedom, every freedom that fails to enter into the whole truth about man and the world" (*RH* 12).

Reflecting further, John Paul II describes freedom as a divine gift and an extraordinary value, provided that we know how to use it correctly. Writing about truth as a condition of freedom, the author highlights the need for courage and readiness to sacrifice oneself, even in the face of persecution. He reminds us that Christ always stands by an internally free person who is capable of defending the truth. The Pope expresses this conviction most eloquently in the following words: "In the course of so many centuries, of so many generations, from the time of the Apostles on, is it not often Jesus Christ himself that has made an appearance at the side of people judged for the sake of the truth? And has he not gone to death with people condemned for the sake of the truth?" (*RH* 12).

Apart from internal freedom as the highest human value, the Pope also considers the question of external freedom as the right of all people. He means here, among other types, the freedom of one's homeland, freedom of opinion, freedom of word, and personal freedom. Unfortunately, the lack of this external freedom characterizes various historical periods, the twentieth century included. Therefore, John Paul II mentions the merits of the UN in the fight for human rights: "We cannot fail to recall at this point . . . the magnificent effort made by the United Nations Organization, an effort conducive to the definition and establishment of man's objective and inviolable rights, with the member States obliging each other to observe them rigorously" (*RH* 17).

Every person entrusted with the gift of freedom can attain salvation in truth, but faces degradation and loss as the consequence of evil choices. The Pope reminds us that Jesus Christ comes to meet people in every age. He comes so as to enlighten us with his truth and thus enables us to give testimony to him in front of others. In those moments of an illuminating encounter, Jesus' words spoken at his trial before Pilate find their confirmation and deepest meaning: "For this I was born and for this I came into the world, to testify to the truth" (Jn 18:37).

John Paul II teaches that to live in a real inner freedom requires on our part vigilant receptiveness to both the internal guidance of the Holy Spirit and to the external assistance of the Church. Understanding the nature of human rights to that freedom can be of help here, and the Pope duly provides his analysis of this situation, which will be presented in the next section.

Human Rights: "Letter" or "Spirit"?

Pope John Paul II points out that the twentieth century has witnessed immense material distraction and moral disintegration. He states that in spite of the existing principles of human rights, as affirmed in the relevant declaration of the United Nations in 1948, the twentieth century has turned out to be a time of moral depravation in society. The Pope calls the twentieth century "a century of great calamities" (*RH* 17) because of this moral depravation, coupled with the annihilation of millions of human beings.

The Holy Father recalls with recognition and gratitude the effort of those who established the United Nations and aimed at preventing the horrors of wars in the first half of the twentieth century from happening again. He appreciates the contribution of the Declaration of Human Rights toward the formation of a better and more just society in the future, as the basis for continued evaluation and necessary revision of worldwide social, economic, political, or cultural programs.

The Pope recognizes with satisfaction that this declaration has been almost universally accepted. Unfortunately, it has not always been implemented in practice, and the Pope recalls an earlier, similar situation in the New Testament. In the Corinthian church, God chose Saint Paul and other leaders "as ministers of a new covenant, not of letter but of spirit; for the letter brings death, but the Spirit gives life" (2 Cor 3:6). Words are spoken, but actions are far from being implemented, so that legislated human rights contrast painfully with the actual situation of people around the globe. The Holy Father emphasizes that the "letter of the law" kills the spirit, while only the spirit gives life. John Paul II ascertains with painful conviction that if "human rights are being violated in various ways, if in practice we see before us concentration camps, violence, torture, terrorism, and discrimination in many forms, this must then be the consequence of the other premises, undermining and often almost annihilating the effectiveness of the humanistic premises of these modern programmes and systems" (*RH* 17).

The author of the encyclical stresses that the Church has always taught the duty to work for common good; and this is a fundamental obligation for all. Authority fulfills its social tasks properly only when it guarantees all citizens their human rights. "The lack of this leads to the dissolution of society, opposition by citizens to authority, or a situation of oppression, intimidation, violence, and terrorism, of which many examples have been provided by the totalitarianisms of this century" (*RH* 17).

John Paul II recognizes that the Church has demanded respect for human rights, especially the right of religious freedom and the freedom of conscience, and these rights are the necessary foundation for people to realize their vocation in Christ. This will be our next subject.

Christian Vocation to Worship and to Serve

Some people relate the word *vocation* to priests and religious alone. Pope John Paul II helps us to see this issue differently. He refers to the teaching of the Second Vatican Council and reminds us that all Christians are called by God to fulfill their proper mission, which depends on their particular vocation. We can speak here about a vocation to the consecrated or religious life, a vocation to family life, or a vocation to single life. A common trait of all these diverse vocations is the call to follow Jesus and to establish a profound friendship with him. Saint Paul says that there is "one body and one Spirit, as you were also called to the one hope of your call" (Eph 4:4). Each one of us discovers his or her specific vocation based on this common Christian calling. It might be a professional vocation as a teacher, doctor, banker, engineer, or baker, to give but a few examples, or a life vocation, like a priest, sculptor, painter, writer, or composer. Let us remember that we can serve God at our best when we integrate our profession with our life vocation.

Later in his encyclical, John Paul II teaches that our participation in the triple mission[1] of Christ—that is, in his office of prophet, priest, and king—is an essential element of our Christian calling (*RH* 18).

Participation in Christ's prophetic mission signifies the communication of God's truth to others as expressed by God in human language. For the laity, this prophetic mission can assume the form of family catechesis (teaching children about God) or of various types of apostolic activity. John Paul II points here in particular to such groups as "those who represent the natural sciences and letters, doctors, jurists, artists and technicians, teachers at various levels and with different specializations. As members of the People of God, they all have their own part to play in Christ's prophetic mis-

---

[1] In the English version of the encyclical *Redeemer of Man*, the triple mission of Christ is described as the "triple office."

sion and service of divine truth, among other ways by an honest attitude towards truth, whatever field it may belong to, while educating others in truth and teaching them to mature in love and justice" (*RH* 19).

Participation in Christ's priestly mission consists in the sacrifice of oneself to God through Jesus Christ as the High Priest. It is imperative here to make a clear distinction between the universal priesthood of lay people and the hierarchical priesthood. The universal priesthood of the laity has its foundation in the sacraments of Baptism and Confirmation. On the basis of these two sacraments, lay people have the right to engage in apostolic activity. Consecrated people, on the other hand, apart from apostolic activity, receive from Christ the right to administer the holy sacraments (Eucharist and Reconciliation in particular) by means of the sacrament of Holy Orders. The author emphasizes that "in Christ, priesthood is linked with his Sacrifice, his self-giving to the Father" (*RH* 20).

The third and last dimension of our mission is the participation in Christ's office as King. This consists in finding "in oneself and others the special dignity of our vocation that can be described as 'kingship'. This dignity is expressed in readiness to serve, in keeping with the example of Christ, who 'came not to be served but to serve'" (*RH* 21, quoting Mt 20:28). The Pope teaches us that the kingship of service is to be expressed in fidelity to a particular vocation, both in matrimony, as a sign of the indissoluble character of the sacramental institution of marriage, and in priesthood, as a sign of "the indelible character that the sacrament of Orders stamps on their souls" (*RH* 21).

The Holy Father turns to Mary the Mother of Jesus and Mother of the Church at the end of his encyclical. This will be the last subject of our summary.

Mary, the Mother of the Church and Our Mother

No comprehensive portrait of Jesus Christ the Redeemer and of his mission in the contemporary world—and the papal encyclical most definitely belongs in this category—can fail to mention Mary, the Mother of the Savior. This is because "the mystery of the Redemption took shape beneath the heart of the Virgin of Nazareth," as John Paul II poetically puts it (*RH* 22). Understandably then, the Pope dedicates the last part of his reflection to the Mother of God.

As an astute theologian, John Paul II recognizes that it is the Church's function to act as the mother to all God's children entrusted to her care. He has described this maternal mission of the Church throughout this encyclical. As a sensitive person, a seasoned catechist, and a caring pastor, however, the Pope is utterly convinced that the Church herself is in need of a mother. He follows in the footsteps of his predecessor Pope Paul VI, who proclaimed Mary to be the Mother of the Church during the Second Vatican Council in 1964, and, as John Paul II observes, "that title has become known far and wide" (*RH* 20).

This last remark may be an allusion to a prolonged debate during that same Vatican Council on the appropriateness of this title. Some bishops preferred to speak of Mary only as the first daughter of the Church, a perfect image of the People of God, or an unsurpassable example to imitate for all believers. Others saw Mary also in relation to her Son's saving mission and called her not only the Mother of the Church but also the Mediatrix (Latin for "female mediator") of all graces, to name but two of the titles. Pope Paul VI accepted the title "Mother of the Church" after the intervention of Cardinal Stefan Wyszyński on behalf of the Polish episcopate. Polish bishops were also the first to institute the feast of Mary the Mother of the Church in 1971, fixing its celebration on a Monday after the Solemnity of Pentecost.

John Paul II returns to the New Testament, where he traces Mary's presence in the life of her Son from the Annunciation to the Crucifixion. It is from the Cross that Jesus "explicitly extended his Mother's maternity in a way that could easily be understood by every soul and every heart" (*RH* 22). The Pope refers here to the episode in the Gospel of John 19:26–27, where Jesus, from the height of his Cross, entrusted to each other's care the Beloved Disciple, John, and his Mother. "Later, all the generations of disciples . . . spiritually took this Mother to their own homes," just as John did in response to Jesus' invitation (*RH* 22).

The Holy Father underlines that Mary was present "when the Church was to be born in visible form" (*RH* 22) on the day of Pentecost in order to spread the Good News of redemption to the ends of the world. This mystery of salvation cannot be completely grasped by the human mind, but it must be assimilated in prayer and contemplation. The Pope expresses the conviction of the whole Church when he confesses that "nobody else can bring us as Mary can into the divine and human dimension of this mystery [because] nobody has been brought into it by God himself as Mary has" (*RH* 22). Contemplation of the mystery of Redemption in the motherly presence of Mary is the surest way to the unity of all Christians so that the message of her Son can reach all humanity.

2 Rich in Mercy (*Dives in Misericordia*)

November 30, 1980

Introduction

MERCY IS OFTEN associated with pity and thus avoided because of the assumed connotations. People prefer to rely on their own individual resources, and on the achievements of technology and science. The practice of mercy in traditional theology is located somewhere between doing good and helping those who are in material or moral need. This approach is justified but not complete. John Paul II presents mercy as a mutual act that consists in a reciprocal exchange of love. We read in his second encyclical that "merciful love is never a unilateral act or process . . . in reality the one who gives . . . can easily find himself in the position of the one who receives, who obtains a benefit, who experiences merciful love; he too can find himself the object of mercy" (*DM* 14).

The author of *Dives in Misericordia* (*Rich in Mercy*) tells us that God reveals his mercy to us most especially when he sees any individual suffering, iniquity among us, or all sorts of physical and moral weaknesses. The Pope emphasizes that this "mode . . . in which love manifests itself . . . in biblical language is called 'mercy'" (*DM* 3).

While reflecting on divine mercy, the Pope highlights the supreme example of Jesus as the One who showed mercy in all his deeds. During his three-year ministry, Jesus expressed the truth of divine mercy through parables. A few of the most well-known are the parables of the Prodigal Son, the Good Shepherd, and the Good Samaritan. The last of these narrates a concrete

13

example of active love toward a man attacked by robbers (Lk 10:30–37). The Samaritan bandaged the wounds of the injured man, brought him to an inn, and assured the necessary care, before continuing his travel.

John Paul II reminds us that the merciful God expects each of us to show an active type of love—mercy, in other words—and this love is to manifest itself in our good deeds and in extending aid to everyone around us. Based on this "loving" understanding of mercy, Jesus proclaims in his Sermon on the Mount: "Blessed are the merciful, for they will be shown mercy" (Mt 5:7).

It is important to note that the author of the encyclical postulates the practice of mercy not only within one's family or neighborhood, but also in wider social contexts, both national and international. Numerous threats that humanity and the world at large face today necessitate this particular type of mercy. Such organizations as the United Nations (UN), the United Nations Educational, Scientific and Cultural Organization (UNESCO), or the Food and Agricultural Organization (FAO) debate the issues of underdevelopment and poverty in various parts of the world. The Pope appreciates the fact that in the contemporary world the sense of social justice has been aroused. In spite of this, many organizations that begin their activity inspired by the idea of justice end up practicing diverse forms of hatred. The Pope sees the lack of love as the root cause of those distortions. He points to the Old Testament principle: " 'An eye for an eye and a tooth for a tooth' (Lev 24:20; Ex 21:24). . . . The experience of the past and of our own time demonstrates that justice alone is not enough, that it can even lead to the negation and destruction of itself, if that deeper power, which is love, is not allowed to shape human life in its various dimensions" (*DM* 12).

Pope John Paul II presents to the only and final means of salvation a humanity faced with extinction, namely, the mystery of God's mercy.

Giving and Forgiving as the Essence of Mercy

John Paul II, while writing the encyclical about the mercy of God, does not define it, but simply points to God himself, since "mercy . . . corresponds . . . to the most profound truth of that love which God is" (*DM* 13). The Pope remarks that the truth about God, who is love and mercy, emerges most perfectly in Christ: "Making the Father present as love and mercy is, in Christ's own consciousness, the fundamental touchstone of His mission as the Messiah" (*DM* 3).

The most telling and touching narrative depicting the merciful love of God to humanity is the parable of the Prodigal Son (Lk 15:11–32). This is the well-known story about the reprehensible behavior of a younger son, who asked his father for his share of the family inheritance and then traveled to a distant country. He lost all his possessions by leading a life of extravagance and debauchery. At the same time, the father never stopped thinking about the son with longing and love, and he suffered greatly as the result of the broken relationship. He thought not so much about the lost property but about his son's dignity and humanity. When he finally saw his younger son returning, he "was filled with compassion. He ran to his son, embraced him and kissed him" (Lk 15:20). The attitude of the father represents the everlasting reality of forgiveness. The son, on the other hand, who was suffering misery as the result of his departure and his loss of dignity, began to miss his father and feel regret for his deplorable behavior. The state of the soul that was formed in the heart of the son is called conversion.

In the attitude of the prodigal son, who occasionally represents each one of us, we can identify two main reasons for his return to his father. Firstly, he wanted to experience the joy of being truly loved by his father. Secondly, he was willing to let his father show him his fatherly love. Even if the son had not returned, the father would have most certainly mercifully forgiven his lost child. The father always remains faithful to himself, and fidelity is connected with mercy. We read in the encyclical that "the father's fidelity to himself is totally concentrated upon the humanity of the lost son, upon his dignity" (*DM* 6).

The father, who constantly waits with the generous gift of forgiveness, also awaits reciprocity. The son must reflect on his behavior and answer the question about his ability to extend his love to his father. If he fails to discover this capability, he needs to repent.

Meanwhile, the elder son had become angry with his wasteful younger brother. He was not willing to accept his father's invitation to rejoice over the return of his brother. He went further and reproached his father for not organizing a party for him and his friends, the way the father did for the repenting brother, even though he himself had never broken any family rules nor left the father even for a moment. The elder son was convinced about his perfection and closed his heart to forgiveness as a result. Blinded by pride, he did not open his heart to his brother, whom the father had already forgiven. The father of the parable treats his sons equally and fairly, just as God treats each one of us equally and fairly and shows his mercy to everyone, even one as weak and morally depraved as the prodigal son.

From this portion of the papal encyclical, related to forgiveness, we are able to find wise suggestions that can be applied in our own lives. It is important to remember that it is not important how far we have strayed from God. He always awaits our return, and when we return, we will experience his embracing arms and kiss. Then our hearts will be filled with peace and joy. A further result will be an increase in love that will be demonstrated in our forgiveness of others and leniency with others' faults.

Reciprocating God's Mercy

John Paul II expounds great truths related to God's mercy in his encyclical. He explains that people are able to show mercy to others only if they have experienced God's mercy themselves. We receive this mercy when God forgives us our sins. God grants us pardon so as to build and strengthen our humanity and restores to our love that creative power through which we recover "access to the fullness of life and holiness that come from God" (*DM* 7). Thanks to God's mercy, we do not fall into despair as the result of moral loss or physical suffering.

God's mercy expressed in the forgiveness of sins cannot be bought by means of fasting, self-sacrifice, or offerings toward noble purposes. The reception of God's mercy begins with conversion of the heart. The Pope expresses this idea as follows: "Man attains to the merciful love of God, His mercy, to the extent that he himself is interiorly transformed in the spirit of that love towards his neighbor. This authentically evangelical process is not just a spiritual transformation realized once and for all: it is a whole lifestyle" (*DM* 14).

Those who help others in their needs (however small and insignificant) with the intention of restoring their human dignity and enabling the deprived to become more fully human imitate God and merit his mercy. Jesus himself assured us when he said, "Blessed are the merciful, for they will be shown mercy" (Mt 5:7).

Mercy has personal character because it involves the meeting of God with a human being, or a meeting among humans. Mercy in a human relationship should manifest itself in real and responsible love. This love is to be offered for its own sake, and not for the sake of some gain, praise, or pleasure. Every human need was the object of Christ's care, as his deeds on earth clearly indicate. Christ himself became a gift for every human being. The Greeks, to give just one example, did not know God as a selfless gift to humanity. Their gods loved people only when the latter provided for their divine needs. True understanding of God's mercy should express itself after the example of Christ as "gift," respecting all that is human in another person. The Pope emphasizes that "mercy is manifested in its true and proper aspect when it restores to value, promotes and draws good from all the forms of evil existing in the world and in man" (*DM* 6).

Yet another dimension of mercy toward our neighbors to whom we wish to show our love (like the father in the parable toward his lost son) is leniency and patience toward errors. Notice that the father waited patiently for his son's return; he waited until his child had reflected upon his evil behavior and desired to return home. The son wanted to reconcile with God and his family so as to receive forgiveness and the peace of mind stemming from a pure conscience. The patience practiced while we await the correction of human misdeeds should be motivated by the desire to rescue what is good in those who do evil. The father of the prodigal son, who strived to rescue his child's dignity and humanity, should be our model.

The conclusion of our reflection is clear: mercy touches human sin. In order to be merciful, we need to know how to be humble, and to always trust, believe, and be absolutely convinced that God's mercy has no end, and is always patient and kind (see 1 Cor 13:4).

Justice and Mercy

The desire to uncover and recover every potential good from under the multiple layers of evil in each person is an amazing feature of this encyclical about God's mercy. Based on his deep understanding of the contemporary crisis of values, the Pope emphasizes the necessity to "connect" love with justice. He observes with concern that modern culture is characterized by "the decline of many fundamental values, which constitute an unquestionable good not only for Christian morality but simply for human morality, for moral culture: these values include respect for human life from the moment of conception, respect for marriage in its indissoluble unity, and respect for the stability of the family" (*DM* 12).

The Holy Father teaches that justice alone as the fundamental principle of social life is not sufficient. He is convinced that our modern world can become more humane only when love and mercy coexist with justice, and all three together permeate human relationships. Yet, the forgiveness that restores humanity and the love that affirms the person do not overturn the objective demands of justice. The criterion of justice is equity and not some absolute and abstract equality, as maintained by the supporters of unjust social and political systems. What is equitable and what is rightly due to everyone is just.

The concept of mercy has been distorted since the nineteenth century when it condoned social inequality among people. The one who was offering (alms to the poor, for example) maintained a higher status than the one who was receiving the gift. In this encyclical, John Paul II does not employ these terms, which are still common today. He does not want to identify mercy with almsgiving, especially when the latter is not offered from a pure heart. Similar acts of kindness are very useful when we perform them from a position as an "equal" to the receiver. When we remain open to accept the "wealth" of the one who receives, this wealth is his or her humanity. The Pope, while talking about mercy, emphasizes human dignity, which he places above simple pity.

When making a reference to redemption, that is, to the forgiveness of human sins by the death of Jesus on the Cross, the Pope writes: "In the passion and death of Christ—in the fact that the Father did not spare His own Son . . . —absolute justice is expressed. . . . [T]his justice, which is properly justice 'to God's measure,' springs completely from love . . . and completely bears fruit in love" (*DM* 7).

God, who is the merciful Father, enters into the concrete history of every person in order to bend low over his or her sin, hatred, and failure. God is just because he gives everyone his or her due in the created world as it actually is. In the relationship between God and humanity, love always precedes justice. The Pope explains this idea in the following words: "Love is 'greater' than justice: greater in the sense that it is primary and fundamental. Love, so to speak, conditions justice and, in the final analysis, justice serves love. The primacy and superiority of love vis-à-vis justice—this is a mark of the whole of revelation—are revealed precisely through mercy" (*DM* 4).

In his encyclical, John Paul II draws particular attention to the human dignity of a person. Those who are guided only by justice can enter into relationships exclusively on the level of material things. Those who include love in their human relationships, instead, can communicate as persons. Having this understanding of a relationship in mind, the Pope teaches that mercy is the source of justice.

God's Mercy in the History of Salvation

John Paul II states that God has shown his mercy to humanity through all ages, but most particularly in the call of Abraham and the covenant with the Chosen People. The Pope formulates this idea as follows: "In deeds and in words, the Lord revealed His mercy from the very beginnings of the people which He chose for Himself; and, in the course of its history, this people continually entrusted itself, both when stricken with misfortune and when it became aware of its sin, to the God of mercies" (*DM* 4).

The Bible describes concrete proofs of God's mercy toward people of all times in both the Old and New Testaments. We learn from the Old Testament about God's mercy revealed in the creation of the world and of the human race, and in God's election of his Chosen People. Other proofs of God's mercy include the liberation of Israel from Egyptian slavery and feeding the escapees in the desert on their way to the Promised Land. The books of the Old Testament depict God's mercy in a social dimension alone. The Pope remarks: "Israel was, in fact, the people of the covenant with God, a covenant that it broke many times. Whenever it became aware of its infidelity—and in the history of Israel there was no lack of prophets and others who awakened this awareness—it appealed for mercy" (*DM* 4).

As he continues his reflection in the encyclical, John Paul underlines that the mercy of God in the New Testament still embraces the Chosen People as a society, but his mercy relates separately to every individual as well. This mercy is connected with "the mystery of the election, which in a special way shaped the history of the people whose spiritual father is Abraham by virtue of his faith. Nevertheless, through this people . . . that mystery of election refers to every man and woman" (*DM* 4).

In the New Testament, God's mercy was most comprehensively manifested by Christ. His life is presented as a vivid example of mercy, while this mercy is never reduced to a mere moral precept. We learn from the encyclical that God's mercy toward humanity was expressed most completely in the three dimensions of Christ's life: in his three-year-long proclamation of the Good News of salvation; in his miracles; and in his Passion, Death, and Resurrection for the salvation of humanity.

While proclaiming the gospel, Jesus expressed the care of the merciful God for humanity in many parables. This care is a manifestation of God's love, and it occurs in human relationships as well. If somebody truly loves another, he does not seek privileges or advantages for himself. Christ himself made a blueprint for such selfless love when he bestowed the priceless gift of himself upon humanity.

Jesus performed miracles in response to human needs. In one case, he multiplied bread and managed to feed a huge crowd of people who listened to him in the desert. Another proof of Jesus' wonderful generosity was the catching of fish. After a night of fruitless labor, Peter and his companions filled two boats with fish, thanks to the intervention of Jesus. Peter was amazed at this feat and began to recognize that Jesus was someone special. He was thus prepared to hear the Master's invitation to embrace a new vocation of "catching" people.

The Cross of Christ: The Source of Mercy

While reflecting on the theme of mercy in his encyclical, the Pope draws our attention to the Paschal Mystery, that is, to Jesus' suffering in Gethsemane, his death on Calvary, and his Resurrection, as the highest revelation of God's mercy to humanity. "The cross is the most profound condescension of God to man and to what man—especially in difficult and painful moments—looks on as his unhappy destiny" (*DM* 8). Through his Cross, Jesus touches the most painful wounds of human earthly existence. God the Redeemer desires in his mercy to spare us suffering in this life and save us from eternal damnation in the next.

When Jesus was condemned to death—when he was derided, flogged, and crowned with thorns—in this most difficult moment, his friends failed him. Precisely when he needed their mercy the most, when evil people crucified him, his closest disciples left him. They left him alone in his sufferings, even though he loved them until the end, until his death. Although he was God, Jesus cried to his Father in terrible loneliness and abandonment:

"My God, my God, why have you forsaken me?" (Mt 27:46). His closest friends forgot that "God is love" (1 Jn 4:8). Jesus' suffering was much deeper. He suffered most of all because his love had been rejected, and love cannot exist all alone. Love left to itself suffers; it does not want anything for itself, and therefore "it does not seek its own interests" (1 Cor 13:5).

John Paul II teaches in his encyclical: "Believing in the crucified Son means . . . believing that love is present in the world and that this love is more powerful than any kind of evil in which individuals, humanity, or the world are involved. Believing in this love means believing in mercy" (*DM* 7). Love is united with forgiveness, and therefore Jesus from the height of his Cross intercedes for his oppressors, crying: "Father, forgive them, they know not what they do" (Lk 23:34). Writing about the forgiving Jesus, the Pope presents forgiveness as the best cure for the wounded hearts of contemporary people, regardless of the origin—whether it is to be found in hatred, malice, pride, foolishness, stubbornness, fear, or any other evil. The Pope points to Jesus who comes out to meet sin and suffering and assures us that, thanks to his mercy, all obstacles can be overcome.

We tend to feel better in the presence of a winner than in the company of someone who suffers. The suffering of Jesus proved to be the way to victory, however. Similarly, those who live according to the truth and proclaim the truth to others ultimately triumph. Sometimes they may be falsely accused and condemned to suffer. Yet those who are ready to suffer for the sake of truth always claim a moral victory, even at the cost of their lives, after the example of Christ and the martyrs. We should never abandon those who suffer for the sake of truth, as their suffering may affect our liberation, as well as our rights.

Jesus, when he was dying on the Cross, opened wide his heart, and thus bestowed his mercy on every human being. We can say that the source of God's mercy "flows" directly from the Cross to the sacrament of Penance that Jesus instituted after his Resurrection, when he said: "Receive the holy Spirit. Whose sins you forgive are forgiven them, and whose sins you retain are retained" (Jn 20:22–23).

Mary, Mother of Mercy

John Paul II did not forget to mention Mary when reflecting on God's mercy in his encyclical. She accompanied Jesus during his entire earthly life. Understandably, the Pope honors Mary with the title "Mother of Mercy." He explains that the apostles and other companions of Jesus were only witnesses of the saving events of Jesus' life, while Mary participated in the life of her Son as his Mother; she could thus claim a share in God's mercy. John Paul II conveyed this idea in these poignant words: "No one has experienced, to the same degree as the Mother of the crucified One, the mystery of the cross. . . . No one has received into his heart, as much as Mary did, that mystery. . . . Mary, then, is the one who has the deepest knowledge of the mystery of God's mercy. She knows its price, she knows how great it is. In this sense, we call her the Mother of mercy; our Lady of mercy; or Mother of divine mercy; in each one of these titles there is a deep theological meaning" (*DM* 9).

During her visit to Saint Elizabeth, Mary expressed her joy at becoming the Mother of the Son of God and praised the Creator in the words of the Magnificat: "My soul proclaims the greatness of the Lord; my spirit rejoices in God my savior. For he has looked upon his handmaid's lowliness; behold, from now on will all ages call me blessed. The Mighty One has done great things for me . . ." (Lk 1:46–49). In this way, Mary the Mother of God became the Mother of the Patriarchs, Prophets, Apostles, and also the Mother of Mercy for all those who believe in her Son. It is primarily to her that sinners pray when they expect mercy in the form of grace, understanding, forgiveness, help, or support. They ask her to intercede with her Son on their behalf.

In concluding the encyclical on God's mercy, Pope John Paul II addresses all who believe in God as follows: "We raise our voices and pray that the Love which is in the Father may once again be revealed at this stage of history. . . . We pray for this through the intercession of her who does not cease to proclaim 'mercy . . . from generation to generation,' and also through the intercession of those for whom there have been completely fulfilled the words of the Sermon on the Mount: 'blessed are the merciful, for they shall obtain mercy'" (*DM* 15). Let us then be merciful toward all people every day and in every circumstance. Let us show mercy in particular to those who are physically or morally weak.

3 On Human Work
(*Laborem Exercens*)

September 14, 1981

Introduction

THE MAIN MESSAGE of the third encyclical of John Paul II, *On Human Work* (*Laborem Exercens*), focuses on the fate of humanity engaged in creating a world by means of economic activity. Its author considers not only the entire heritage of the Church's social teaching but also new realities that influence and shape human work. It is significant that this encyclical appeared on the ninetieth anniversary of *Rerum Novarum*, the first social encyclical of Pope Leo XIII, which had been published in 1891.

Among the new issues related to human work upon which John Paul II reflects are the moral aspects of work and its personal character. The Pope strongly emphasizes that human work cannot be treated as a thing, a commodity, or a means to gain power and control over other people. Work is a vocation for every human being, an inexhaustible source of self-improvement and personal growth. We can participate in God's creative activity by means of our work, in accordance with his command to "subdue" the earth (see Gen 1:28). In this way, we make the world perfect—more beautiful, just, and humane.

While considering the numerous aspects of human work, the Holy Father draws our attention to its arduousness. He recalls God's words to the first couple after their fall, speaking of thorns and thistles that would make tilling the ground difficult and of the hardships that would accompany food-gathering (see Gen 3:17–19). Those words of God, harsh as they seem to be, do not transform human work into a form of penance or punishment for sins, as some falsely maintain. The biblical story of Adam and Eve conveys the truth that human work became harder as the consequence of breaking God's law. John Paul II addresses humanity overburdened with work and points to a higher, supernatural sense of work in the following words: "Sweat and toil, which work necessarily involves the present condition of the human race, present the Christian and everyone who is called to follow Christ with the possibility of sharing lovingly in the work that Christ came to do (see Jn 17:4). This work of salvation came about through suffering and death on a Cross. By enduring the toil of work in union with Christ crucified for us, man in a way collaborates with the Son of God for the redemption of humanity" (*LE* 27).

The author of this encyclical on human work speaks also about the immense dignity of the working person, regardless of the type of work in which he or she is engaged. The more love we put into our work, the greater our sense of dignity. No work degrades us, because God does not evaluate us on the basis of the type of work that we do, but rather on our commitment, diligence, and honesty in fulfilling our tasks. In God's eyes, the work of a street-sweeper is equally valuable and important as that of a university professor, provided it is carried out diligently and with love for those it is meant to serve. We can thus say that human work is a sort of benchmark for the value of a person. Christ himself invokes this criterion: "by their fruits you will know them" (Mt 7:16).

While showing the true value of work, the Pope warns the contemporary world against objectification and depersonalization of human work, which degrade our humanity. He teaches that God calls us to accomplish a triple mission by means of our work: personal self-realization, creation of a unifying community, and cultivation of "God's garden."

Praise for Industriousness

Before Karol Wojtyla became priest, bishop, cardinal, and finally Pope, he used to work physically as a quarryman in Zakrzowek (1940), then at Solvay Chemical in a water purification plant (1941). In this way, he came to know all types of work, including manual labor. The Pope is convinced that the issues of working people with which he deals in his encyclical cannot be correctly presented without reference to the gospel. Therefore, he speaks about the "Gospel of work" and points to Christ, who in spite of being God "devoted most of the years of his life on earth to *manual work* at the carpenter's bench" (*LE* 6).

John Paul II exalts work by calling it a good for any person, and a good for our humanity. Therefore, he calls industriousness a virtue, that is, a moral habit, a moral competence: "something whereby man becomes good as man" (*LE* 9).

The Bible, the main source of the Holy Father's inspiration, praises industriousness and condemns laziness. A lazy person is portrayed in the Old Testament not only as useless but also as socially harmful. An idler is most strongly criticized when he spends money, while a common good, on his own pleasures. In the Book of Proverbs, its writer gives examples from nature to shame those lazy loafers: "Go to the ant, O sluggard, study her ways . . . ; For though she has no chief, no commander or ruler, she procures her food in the summer, stores up her provisions in the harvest" (Prov 6:6–8). In Proverbs we also have praise of industriousness: a worthy wife, who provides for the needs of the family and even those of the servants through her hard work, is given as a positive example to imitate (see Prov 31:10–31). The woman was praised not only for providing her family with the necessities of life, but also for the fact that her family members, thanks to her work, could earn the respect of others and enhance their social status.

It is obvious to the Pope that we should be completely—physically, psychologically, and emotionally—involved in the work that we do. We do not work with our hands or minds alone. Work is an act of a complete human being and has personal character. We have received two precious gifts from God: hands to work and intellect to think. By applying these gifts industriously, we create our own welfare and grow spiritually. The Pope describes a working person as the one who "performs various actions belonging to the work process; independently of their objective content, these actions must all serve to realize his humanity, to fulfill the calling to be a person that is his by reason of his very humanity" (*LE* 6). By means of our work, we are to "subdue" the earth (see Gen 1:28) since, as John Paul II says, "in carrying out this mandate . . . every human being . . . reflects the very action of the Creator of the universe" (*LE* 4).

Industriousness does not mean "being lost" in work, or lacking time for others, especially family and friends, as well as those who need us. We must set aside time for rest and time for God.

Each individual theme that the Pope treats here should be understood in the context of his entire teaching. Presenting God's action as a model of human activity is a central idea in John Paul II's teachings: "Therefore man's work too not only requires a rest every 'seventh day,' (Deut 5:12–14; Ex 20:8–12) but also . . . it must leave room for man to prepare himself, by becoming more and more what in the will of God he ought to be, for the *'rest' that the Lord reserves for his servants and friends* (Mt 25:21; *LE* 25).

Creativity and Dignity at Work

When God created man, he gave each a task to multiply and subdue the earth (Gen 1:28). The Pope notes that "even though these words do not refer directly and explicitly to work, beyond any doubt they indirectly indicate it as an activity for man to carry out in the world" (*LE* 4). John Paul II vehemently rejects contemporary materialistic trends, which reduce a human being to a lifeless machine. He reminds us that "man's work concerns not only the economy but also, and especially, personal values" (*LE* 15). He also disapproves of classifying work as creative or non-creative, nor as appropriate for a free person or slave. These types of categorizations existed since antiquity, were valid in the Greco-Roman world, and were held to be true even in Christianity, which failed to break free from them for centuries. For many generations, only masterpieces of art like painting, sculpture, or literature were deemed worthy of being called creative work.

As a result of the above misconceptions about work, many people today still treat their activities quite mechanically and superficially. They evaluate them purely in terms of gain and immediate effects, while renouncing creativity and higher aspirations. The Pope believes that creative work needs an appropriate system of values, symbols, and meanings, because all the elements that constitute a human being—material and spiritual, temporary and eternal—are involved in the creative process. Every human being created in God's image and likeness has been equipped with these elements as a person. God and humanity become partners in the creative process, since God invites us to share in his creative work. Those who attain a high level of spiritual development are capable of creating material goods of the highest quality.

The Pope insists that while considering human creativity we must not forget the fact that we are persons, and as such we are the subjects of our work; this fact determines the value and dignity of all our activities. These activities include both the most modest and menial, as well as those most elevated and noble. The type of activity is ultimately not important but "the fact that the one who carries it out is a person" (*LE* 6). There are, of course, many forms of human activity related to the variety of professions and needs that exist in a given historical period and culture.

John Paul II strongly defends the dignity of working people and of their creative potential, regardless of the level of technological development of their civilization. The Pope explains that even when a worker operates a machine that actually produces various material objects, it is still the work of a person who is creative, because only the working person uses his or her freedom and reason, gifts the machine does not possess.

The term *work* is attributed to a person and not to a machine. The Pope justifies this statement in the following words: "The development of industry and of the various sectors connected with it, even the most modern electronics technology, especially in the fields of miniaturization, communications and telecommunications and so forth, show how vast is the role of technology, that ally of work that human thought has produced. . . . [Technology] understood in this case not as a capacity or aptitude for work, but rather as a *whole set of instruments* which man uses in his work" (*LE* 5).

Regardless of the level of technological development, however, a person with his or her creative potential remains the only one to inspire, create, recreate, renew, perfect, and enrich all the various facets and spheres of life: material and spiritual, personal and social. Creativity, namely, is the most unique gift of God to humanity.

The Rights of Working People

John Paul II notes that human work has many aspects. Thanks to work, men and women master the material world, transform nature, gain the means to survive, cooperate with God, and develop spiritually. The Pope speaks also about the duty to work based on the command of the Creator:

"Man must work, both because the Creator has commanded it and because of his own humanity, which requires work in order to be maintained and developed. Man must work out of regard for others, especially his own family, but also for the society he belongs to, the country of which he is a child, and the whole human family of which he is a member, since he is the heir to the work of generations and at the same time a sharer in building the future of those who will come after him in the succession of history" (*LE* 16).

The Bible, the main source of the Pope's teaching, contains numerous texts about the necessity of human work. Saint Paul states very strongly that "if anyone was unwilling to work, neither should that one eat" (2 Thes 3:10). What the apostle means is that those who do not want to work have no moral right to be maintained by those who do work.

The Pope speaks not only about the duty to work but also about the rights of those who do work. He considers the relationship between an employed person and his or her employer, making a clear distinction between a direct and an indirect employer. The direct employer is the person or institution with whom a work contract is signed. As for the indirect employer, the Pope cites "many different factors, other than the direct employer, that exercise a determining influence on the shaping . . . of the work contract" (*LE* 16).

John Paul II deals with the various factors that determine the employment of workers. He defends the right of workers to organize trade unions in order to defend their rights as employees in matters related to working conditions, correct employment policies, or just compensation. Those factors also involve political parties, labor laws of individual states, as well as international economic and financial institutions. The Holy Father gives special ideas: "Workers can often share in running businesses and in controlling their productivity, and in fact do so. Through appropriate associations, they exercise influence over conditions of work and pay, and also over social legislation" (*LE* 8).

Keeping his experience of work in a Solvay factory in mind, John Paul II highlights the discrimination against workers during the Nazi occupation of Poland. Years later, as Pope, he warns against the dangers that workers face in all political and social systems. Thus he shows workers the way to self-organization, and the creation of trade unions and of other civil institutions in order to defend their interests and rights.

We need to stress here the Pope's firm stance on the side of a working person and his or her dignity: "Movements of solidarity in the sphere of work—a solidarity that must never mean being closed to dialogue and collaboration with others—can be necessary also with reference to the condition of social groups that were not previously included in such movements. . . . This solidarity must be present whenever it is called for by the social degrading of the subject of work, by exploitation of the workers and by the growing areas of poverty and even hunger" (*LE* 8).

Priority of Labor over Capital

Apart from the personal character of work and its moral aspects, Pope John Paul II in this encyclical deals also with the relation between labor and capital. He firmly supports the priority of labor in this relationship. In order to clarify his position, the Pope refers to its historical origins. He recalls the Industrial Revolution, which started in the second half of the eighteenth century in Great Britain, when machines began to replace people, and "labor was separated from capital and set in opposition to it" (*LE* 13).

This development also brought about many changes in the psyche of the worker. Up to the Industrial Revolution, an artisan's work had a holistic character, since the same person designed, developed, refined, and fabricated an end item in his own workshop, thus carrying out work from beginning to end. Factory work presupposes the division of labor, and its fragmentation into individual activities often done by machines alone. It is very hard for someone who performs a simple, isolated task designed by someone else to see a social dimension in his or her work. Work on a production line easily causes boredom and psychological fatigue. Machines are not adapted to a worker, and so the worker has to adjust to the machine. The duty of an employee is simply to handle the machine, with the latter being more important in a factory than the person who takes care of it. We can say that mechanization reduced the value of qualified workers, whose place was taken by those merely trained to attend machines.

The most important new element that appeared with the Industrial Revolution was the proletariat, a class of people who did not possess income-generating property or their own workshops (the word *proletariat* derives from the Latin *proles*, "a child," and in ancient Rome denoted the lowest social class). The main source of income for the proletariat was work in plants and factories. The owners of those factories, that is, the owners of a new type of capital previously limited to land, became dictators of the proletariat. The Pope observes that *"the issue of ownership of property* enters from the beginning into the whole of this difficult historical process"* (*LE* 14).

The Pope reminds us that Church teaching

> *diverges* radically from the program of *collectivism* as proclaimed by Marxism and put into practice in various countries. . . . At the same time it differs from the program of *capitalism* practiced by liberalism and by the political systems inspired by it. In the latter case, the difference consists in the way the right to ownership or property is understood. . . . Furthermore, in the Church's teaching, ownership has never been understood in a way that could constitute grounds for social conflict in labor. Property is acquired first of all through work in order that it may serve work. (*LE* 14)

Because work is assigned to a person, the conclusion is simple: capital must serve the worker. The Pope is firm in this: "The *principle of the priority of labor* over capital is a postulate of the order of social morality. . . . Man's work concerns not only the economy but also, and especially, personal values" (*LE* 15).

Catholic Social Teaching on Human Work

The term "Catholic social teaching" was employed for the first time by Pope Pius XI in his Encyclical *Quadragesimo Anno* (*The Fortieth Year*) issued in 1931, the fortieth anniversary of the Encyclical *Rerum Novarum*. In some countries, alternative names have been used, such as "social teaching of the Church," "social issues," or "Catholic social ethics." Catholic social teaching has two main sources: (1) those of a religious nature—a combination of the Bible, the Fathers of the Church, and the teachings of the popes; and (2) those of a secular nature—that is, sociology, economics, law, politics, and other social sciences.

Despite the fact that human work became the subject of Catholic social teaching only in the nineteenth century, it was always present in the background of Christ's instructions and the *kerygma* (Greek word meaning "proclamation," referring to the teaching that Jesus is the Messiah) of the early Church. The Pope underlines this continuity: "Work is one of these aspects, a perennial and fundamental one, one that is always relevant and constantly demands renewed attention and decisive witness" (*LE* 1).

The Christians in the early centuries did not separate religious and secular spheres of life. The two aspects of reality were integrated in such a way that they produced a unified individual and social morality. The disassociation of religious and secular spheres of life took place later, during the Enlightenment. Human involvement in social life was considered to be a purely secular phenomenon, and thus off limits to religion. During the period of intense secularization, the epochs of the Reformation and the Enlightenment in particular, the ways of the Church and of the state split. Those changes provided the Catholic Church with an opportunity to develop her social doctrine in a more comprehensive manner to include a whole new range of social issues.

The Church began to teach on social issues, including human work, in a systematic way toward the end of the nineteenth century, and she continues to do it today. John Paul II reiterates his belief that "the Church considers it her task always to call attention to the dignity and rights of those who work, to condemn situations in which that dignity and those rights are violated, and to help to guide the above-mentioned changes so as to ensure authentic progress by man and society" (*LE* 1). He does not specify detailed solutions of social questions related to human work in various socioeconomic systems. The moral principles that he upholds, however, always aim at defending the personal dignity of workers and at guaranteeing their inviolable rights. The Pope is convinced "that human work is a *key*, probably *the essential key*, to the whole social question, if we try to see that question really from the point of view of man's good" (*LE* 3).

Prayer and Spiritual Growth through Work

The personal character of work, a motif often mentioned by John Paul II in his encyclical, is naturally linked with spiritual growth. When we keep in mind our cooperation in the creative activity of God, we can perfect ourselves through work. The attitude of Martha, who was taking care of household duties when Jesus visited her house, is frequently contrasted with that of her sister, Mary, who was listening attentively to Jesus' every word at the same time. But both the Bible and John Paul II's encyclical depict prayer and work as elements that complement each other, while fostering the spiritual growth of a person. The Pope's words can serve as a good example of this conviction: "When a man works he not only alters things and society, he develops himself as well" (*LE* 26).

The author of the encyclical reminds working people to uphold the Christian hierarchy of values, which constitute the necessary condition of spiritual growth. He expresses this idea in the following words: "Especially in the modern age, the *spirituality* of work should show the *maturity* called for by the tensions and restlessness of mind and heart" (*LE* 25) He stresses with particular force the need to remember "the truth that by means of work man participates in the activity of God himself" (*LE* 26).

John Paul II points to Jesus as the supreme model of balance between work and prayer. Since Christ gave us the example of humble prayer and diligent work, our profound union with him should allow us to learn from him about both prayer and work. Jesus himself invited workers in the following words: "Come to me, all you who labor and are burdened, and I will give you rest. Take my yoke upon you and learn from me, for I am meek and humble of heart; and you will find rest for yourselves" (Mt 11:28–29).

Calling to mind the Bible and all the Christian traditions that deal with human work, the Pope evokes the beautiful Benedictine rule, *ora et labora* (Latin for "pray and work"). This rule describes the work of the Creator, about whom Jesus in the Gospel of John says, "My Father is at work until now, so I am at work" (Jn 5:17). It also applies to the work of Christ the Redeemer, who looks with love at every human effort.

John Paul's teaching about the spiritual and prayer-related elements of human work can best be summarized in the words of Saint Paul: "Whatever you do, do from the heart, as for the Lord and not for others, knowing that you will receive from the Lord the due payment of the inheritance" (Col 3:23–24).

The Eternal Dimension of Human Work

In the last chapter of his encyclical on work, John Paul II observes: "The Christian finds in human work a small part of the Cross of Christ," and "by enduring the toil of work in union with Christ . . . man in a way collaborates with the Son of God for the redemption of humanity" (*LE* 27). In terms of our daily life, this means that Jesus, who died and rose from the dead for us, acts on and through us when we unite our work with the sacramental life of the Church. In this sense, our human work has an eternal dimension.

The Pope clearly aims at presenting comprehensively all aspects of human work in relation to both earthly and divine realms. We should always see the link between the creative activity of God and the saving activity of Christ. We have a share in this unfathomable and marvelous mystery of God when we participate in Holy Mass.

It is precisely in the Eucharist that human work is sanctified by its union with the worship that we offer to God. Bread and wine, the fruits of human work transformed into the Body and Blood of the Lord by God's power, become the spiritual food of a working person. When workers maintain their closeness to divine reality through their participation in Holy Mass, and to earthly reality through their work, it is much easier for them to hear the great hymn of praise that the hearts of other workers sing in their love for God, where all find their true selves.

Apart from the religious dimensions of the Eucharist and human work, we need to bear in mind their profoundly human sense. During Holy Liturgy, the fruits of human work are offered primarily, but not exclusively, to God; other people benefit from them as well. It is particularly during Mass that we realize that the products of our work are useful and beneficial to our neighbors. In this manner, our work inspires and enflames our love of neighbor in God. Just as we exchange the sign of peace at Mass, we should respect each other in our places of work. We cannot possibly work with a clenched fist and a closed heart.

Only when we participate in the Eucharist with utmost commitment are we being redeemed, and our work acquires an eternal dimension. The Pope urges us on: "Let the Christian who listens to the word of the living God, uniting work with prayer, know the place that his work has not only in *earthly progress*, but also in *the development of the kingdom of God*, to which we are all called through the power of the Holy Spirit and through the word of the Gospel" (*LE* 27).

4 The Apostles of the Slavs (*Slavorum Apostoli*)

June 2, 1985

Introduction

I N 1980, two years into his pontificate, Pope John Paul II drew the attention of the world to the evangelizing work of Cyril and Methodius, the Brothers from Salonika (ancient Thessalonica) in Greece, who planted the gospel of Christ among the Slav nations. It was then that the Holy Father proclaimed them, together with Saint Benedict from Nursia, co-patrons of Europe.

Five years later, in 1985, the Holy Father devoted a new encyclical to the lives and work of these eminent missionaries and entitled it *Slavorum Apostoli* (*The Apostles of the Slavs*), a title that fully reflects the character of the evangelizing and apostolic activity of the two saints. Publication of both the co-patrons' document and the encyclical must be seen as salient events of the pontificate of the Pope of Slav origins.

A prophetic vision for a Slav pope was written over 150 years ago by the Polish poet Juliusz Slowacki, and it gains new significance in view of these events. We need to remember that John Paul II was always proud of his Slav origins and culture. On the eleventh centenary of Saint Methodius's death (February 14, 885), the Pope emphasized the importance of his mission in relation to that of the two apostles by issuing his encyclical on that date. He humbly admitted that "a particular obligation . . . is felt by the first Pope called to the See of Peter from Poland" (*SA* 3).

The central theme of this fourth papal encyclical—about the Apostles of the Slavs—is the unity of Europe based on Christian values. The exceptional wisdom of Saints Cyril and Methodius is most evident in noting how they maintained communion with Rome while respecting the culture of the nations they were evangelizing. The two had been brought up in the tradition of Eastern Christianity and represented the Church of Constantinople, which differed culturally from the Western Church. Those differences were particularly marked in the liturgy and the administrative structures of the two churches. The Western Church (western and central Europe) used logic and reason to convey the Word of God, while her administrative structures were neatly ordered on the basis of Roman legal traditions. The ancient Oriental culture (that is, the Eastern Christian tradition), on the other hand, was distinguished by mysticism and intuition. The two trends of the Christian tradition mutually complemented each other and unified Europe as one cultural whole.

In his encyclical addressed to the universal Church, John Paul II intended to point out to contemporary Europe, which remains socially, religiously, and politically divided, that Christianity is the source of its unity. It was on the European continent that human rights were first formulated on the basis of Christian values. While reflecting on the missionary work of Saints Cyril and Methodius, the Pope underlines that spiritual unity based on the gospel is a guarantee of respect for linguistic and cultural variety.

In the spirit of such unity, Cyril and Methodius opened up new areas in their missionary work. The Pope stressed that the two "were . . . not afraid to use the Slavonic language in the liturgy. . . . This they did without any spirit of superiority or domination, but out of love . . . for peoples then developing" (*SA* 12).

The Lives of Saints Cyril and Methodius in Their Historical Context

The brothers Cyril and Methodius were born in the Greek city of Thessalonica (contemporary Salonika), situated on the border of the Slav territories. It was a main cultural, economic, and political center of the Byzantine Empire in the ninth century. It also had its Slavonic name, Solun. The two saints are often called the Brothers from Salonika.

Methodius (probably baptized Michael), the elder of the two, was born between 815 and 820, while the younger, Constantine (better known by his monastic name Cyril), was born in 826. Their father was a senior official of the imperial administration. The two acquired their basic education in Thessalonica but moved to Constantinople to pursue higher learning at the Imperial Academy. Cyril, having been ordained a priest as a young man, became librarian of the archive attached to the Church of Holy Wisdom in Constantinople, and at the same time assumed an influential post as secretary to the patriarch of the city. This brilliant career did not last long, however. He gave up the privileges attached to his status in order to find shelter in a monastery on the coast of the Black Sea. Some six months later, he was persuaded to lecture in philosophy at a school of higher learning in Constantinople, gaining the nickname the Philosopher because of his outstanding knowledge. After a mission to the Saracens, he joined his brother in a monastery (*SA* 4).

Cyril was thus well prepared not only to work in civil administration but also to carry out various diplomatic missions. The same was true of Methodius, who pursued a political career for a while, reaching the rank of archon, or prefect, in a border province inhabited by many Slavs. He gave up this secular career around 840 and joined "one of the monasteries at the foot of Mount Olympus in Bithynia" (*SA* 4). Many years later, around 863, together with his younger brother, he became involved in the evangelizing missions among the Slavs (*SA* 5). After the death of Cyril (in Rome, in 869), Methodius was consecrated Archbishop of Sirmium in Greater Moravia. He died in Valehrad in 885 (*SA* 6).

Cyril and Methodius translated part of the Bible and some liturgical books into the Old Slavonic language in preparation for their evangelizing mission. When Rastilav, the Prince of Greater Moravia, asked Emperor Michael III for missionaries, the two brothers were chosen and sent there, probably by the year 863.

The missionary activity of the brothers from Salonika took place during the separation of European Christianity into East and West, with Constantinople and Rome as respective centers. Two diverse religious, liturgical, and cultural doctrines faced each other in many Slav countries at the time. The wisdom of the two brothers consisted in their ability to combine these two traditions while maintaining religious and cultural unity. The Pope describes their achievements in the following words: "Byzantine in culture, the brothers Cyril and Methodius succeeded in becoming apostles of the Slavs in the full sense of the word. The two holy Brothers had the resources of energy, prudence, zeal and charity needed for bringing the light to the future believers" (*SA* 8 and 9). In spite of their qualities and efforts, the ninth century turned out to be "the beginning of wider divergences, which were unfortunately destined to increase, between Eastern and Western Christianity, and the two holy missionaries found themselves personally involved in this. But they always succeeded in maintaining perfect orthodoxy and consistent attention both to the deposit of tradition and to the new elements in the lives of the peoples being evangelized" (*SA* 10).

The Old Slavonic Language Becomes a New Biblical and Liturgical Language

The missionary work of Cyril and Methodius that laid Christian foundations in the Slav culture broke the tradition of using only Hebrew, Greek, and Latin in Church liturgy and the Bible. The Roman Church, for example, introduced the Latin language and culture in any new territories that entered under her jurisdiction.

The Greco-Byzantine culture of the missionaries from Salonika influenced their evangelization efforts among the Slav peoples. Despite the prominence of that culture at the time, the Brothers from Salonika appreciated the Slav culture as well. They developed a new alphabet, called *glagolica*, for the Old Slavonic language. They had accomplished this task even before their departure to Moravia. The Pope highly rates their work, writing: "the translation of the sacred books, carried out by Cyril and Methodius . . . conferred a capacity and cultural dignity upon the Old Slavonic liturgical language, which became for many hundreds of years not only the ecclesiastical but also the official and literary language, and even the common language of the more educated classes of the greater part of the Slav nations, and in particular of all the Slavs of the Eastern Rite" (*SA* 21).

In spite of a relatively short time for the missionary activities of Cyril and Methodius in Slav territories, the new alphabet of the Old Slavonic language they introduced exerted tremendous influence on the development of Slav culture. The Pope recognizes this fundamental contribution of the language to the culture:

> In the historical development of the Slavs of Eastern Rite, this language played a role equal to that of the Latin language in the West. It also lasted

longer than Latin—in part until the nineteenth century—and exercised a much more direct influence on the formation of the local literary languages, thanks to its close kinship with them.

These merits vis-à-vis the culture of all the Slav peoples and nations make the work of evangelization carried out by Saints Cyril and Methodius in a certain sense constantly present in the history and in the life of these peoples and nations. (*SA* 22)

Inculturation in the Evangelized Slav Territories

Inculturation turned out to be an enduring heritage of the evangelizing work of Cyril and Methodius in the Slav territories. *Inculturation* is to be understood here as the introduction of the gospel to a local culture using the local language, with subsequent approval by the Church. The word *evangelization* means proclaiming the gospel according to Jesus' command "Go, therefore, and make disciples of all nations" (Mt 28:19). John Paul II described the brothers' evangelical work among the Slavs in the following words: "The Brothers from Salonika were not only heirs of the faith but also heirs of the culture of Ancient Greece, continued by Byzantium. . . . The work of evangelization which they carried out as pioneers in territory inhabited by Slav peoples—contains both a model of what today is called "inculturation, the incarnation of the Gospel in native cultures and also the introduction of these cultures into the life of the Church" (*SA* 21).

We must underline here once again that the wisdom of Cyril and Methodius in their evangelical work consisted in maintaining communion with the two Christian and cultural centers, Constantinople and Rome. They made the Churches of East and West meet peacefully because of "their vision of the Church as one, holy and universal" (*SA* 12), as the Holy Father aptly observes. The whole pontificate of Pope John Paul II and his encyclical about the Apostles of the Slavs in particular draw the attention of the world to Eastern Europe. Thanks to the Holy Father, the Brothers from Salonika became models of Christian universalism, which removes barriers, eliminates hate, and unites everyone in Christ's love. The Pope is convinced that these timeless values are extremely important in contemporary society. He says: "For us today their apostolate also possesses the eloquence of an ecumenical appeal: it is an invitation to restore, in the peace of reconciliation, the unity that was gravely damaged after the time of Cyril and Methodius, and, first and foremost, the unity between East and West" (*SA* 13).

When Prince Rastislav asked for missionaries who knew the Slav language, Cyril and Methodius were sent. But when Louis the German defeated Rastislav, Cyril and Methodius fled to Pannonia in 866, where they were welcomed by the Slav Prince Kocel. The two brothers traveled to the seat of the patriarchate in Aquileia to have their followers ordained. Pope Nicholas I invited them to Rome, but it was his successor Pope Hadrian II who actually received them warmly in the capital of Western Christianity and ordained Methodius and his three disciples as priests. Cyril died during this stay in Rome in 869.

Methodius returned to Pannonia first as papal legate, and then as archbishop for the territory of the ancient diocese of Pannonia in Greater Moravia. "The new sovereign of Greater Moravia, Prince Svatopluk, . . . showed hostility to the work of Methodius. He opposed the Slavonic liturgy and spread doubts in Rome about the new Archbishop's orthodoxy" (*SA* 6). Methodius was imprisoned by the German episcopate because of a dispute over territorial jurisdiction and was held until 878 when Pope John VIII intervened on Methodius's behalf. After hearing Methodius's defense in Rome, the same Pope reinstated him as legate for the Slav peoples. The Papal Bull of 880 reintroduced the Slavonic language into the liturgy, but the activity of Methodius continued to be plagued by "journeys, privations, sufferings, hostility and persecution" (*SA* 5).

In view of these tribulations, the following words of John Paul II are fully justified: "Cyril and Methodius are as it were the connecting links or spiritual bridge between the Eastern and Western traditions, which both come together in the one great Tradition of the universal Church" (*SA* 27).

The Slav Pope and the Unity of Europe

In this encyclical, John Paul II outlines his vision for the spiritual unity of Christian Europe and presents it to the universal Church and the world at large. The document is an appeal to our contemporary population of the old continent to do everything to recover its lost unity. The Holy Father presupposes that the evangelical values are the foundation of this unity. He expresses his respect and admiration to the Brothers from Salonika because "they established the Church with an awareness of her universality. . . . It can be said that Jesus' priestly prayer—*Ut Unum Sint* (Jn 17:21)—was their missionary motto" (*SA* 13).

Karol Wojtyla, the first Polish pope, who undertook Slavonic and Polish studies during his university years, prays for the unity of Europe—the continent he was always proud of—at the end of his encyclical with the following words:

O great God, One in Trinity, I entrust to you the heritage of faith of the Slav nations; preserve and bless this work of yours! . . .

Grant, O Father, what the whole Church today implores from you and grant also that the people and the nations which, thanks to the apostolic mission of the holy Brothers from Salonika, have known and accepted you, the true God, and through Baptism have entered into the holy community of your children, may still continue, without hindrance, to accept with enthusiasm and trust this evangelical program and continue to realize all their human possibilities on the foundation of their teachings! . . .

But also grant to the whole of Europe, O Most Holy Trinity, that through the intercession of the two holy Brothers it may feel ever more strongly the need for religious and Christian unity and for a brotherly communion of all its peoples, so that when incomprehension and mutual distrust have been overcome and when ideological conflicts have been conquered in the common awareness of the truth, it may be for the whole world an example of just and peaceful coexistence in mutual respect and inviolate liberty. . . .

The whole Church thanks you, who called the Slav nations into the communion of the faith, for this heritage and for the contribution made by them to the universal patrimony. The Pope of Slav origin in a special way thanks you for this. (*SA* 30 and 31)

5

The Lord and Giver of Life
(*Dominum et Vivificantem*)

May 18, 1986

Introduction

I N HIS FIFTH encyclical, *Dominum et Vivificantem*, Pope John Paul II describes the profound significance of the third Person of the Most Holy Trinity—the Holy Spirit—within the life of the Church and of every human being. The Holy Father sees the Holy Spirit "at the center of the Christian faith" and recognizes him to be "the source and dynamic power of the Church's renewal" (*DV* 2).

The ninetieth anniversary of the first social encyclical of Leo XIII in 1981, and the eleventh centenary of the death of Saint Methodius in 1985, absorbed the attention of the Pope and caused him to write two important encyclicals, *On Human Work* and *The Apostles of the Slavs*, to mark each of these occasions. It is reasonable to conclude that these two anniversaries upset the most logical sequence of papal documents. The current fifth encyclical would have fit perfectly following those dealing with the Son of God, the Redeemer (*Redemptor Hominis*), and with God the Father (*Dives in Misericordia*).

At the very beginning of this encyclical concerning the Holy Spirit, *The Lord and Giver of Life*, the author refers to one symbol of the Catholic faith, the Creed, elaborated and announced at the two Ecumenical Councils of Nicaea (325) and Constantinople (381). Both councils, through the Creed, highlighted the importance of the Holy Spirit to the Church. The Pope reiterates the importance of the teachings about the Holy Spirit as expounded in more recent time, through the Encyclicals *Divinum illud munus* (1897) by Leo XIII and *Mystici Corporis* (1943) of Pius XII, as well as documents of the Second Vatican Council.

Writing about the complexity of the Spirit, the Giver of Life, the Holy Father refers to God's care for the eternal life of people through all time as implemented by the Church. John Paul II emphasizes this truth: "The Church, therefore, instructed by the words of Christ, and drawing on the experience of Pentecost and her own apostolic history, has proclaimed since the earliest centuries her faith in the Holy Spirit, as the giver of life, the one in whom the inscrutable Triune God communicates himself to human beings, constituting in them the source of eternal life" (*DV* 1).

The Holy Spirit is the Giver of Life and is also known as the Spirit of Truth, Advocate, and Paraclete, or Counselor. The Pope reminds us the words of Christ describing the Holy Spirit:

> "But the Counselor, the Holy Spirit, whom the Father will send in my name, he will teach you all things, and bring to your remembrance all that I have said to you" (Jn 14:26). The Holy Spirit will be the Counselor of the Apostles and the Church, always present in their midst—even though invisible—as the teacher of the same Good News that Christ proclaimed. . . . He will help people to understand the correct meaning of the content of Christ's message. . . . The Holy Spirit, then, will ensure that in the Church there will always continue the same truth which the Apostles heard from their Master (*DV* 4).

Other teachings about the Holy Spirit are also discussed. The Spirit is the One who permeated the whole of creation right from the beginning, when he hovered over the waters while God the Father was creating the world. The Spirit is present at every creative act in which God grants a human being an immortal soul. The Spirit is also the One who "will convict the world in regard to sin and righteousness and condemnation" (Jn 16:8). The Pope also discusses the issue of sins against the Holy Spirit, which, unlike other sins, cannot be forgiven, but more about this later. The Pope refers to the words of the Risen Christ—"Receive the holy Spirit. Whose sins you forgive are forgiven them, and whose sins you retain are retained" (Jn 20:22–23)—in order to highlight the role of the Spirit in the sacrament of Penance.

New Life in the Holy Spirit

Pope John Paul II elucidates various elements of the Church's rich doctrine regarding the Holy Spirit. He points to the whole history of salvation, which can be described as the history of God coming ever closer to humanity through the Holy Spirit until our eternal union with him is reached. In this divine plan of history, Jesus Christ is present in the sacraments of the Church by means of the Holy Spirit. Jesus Christ enters into our personal histories as well, yet again through the same Spirit. It is in fact through the Holy Spirit that "the Good News [of Jesus] takes shape in human minds and hearts and extends through history" (see *DV* 64). People filled with the Spirit are able to transform their own life stories into the history of salvation. The Pope points out: "Under the action of the same Spirit, man . . . redeemed by Christ, draw near to their ultimate destinies in God" (*DV* 64). It is hard to imagine a function greater and nobler than that.

In the introduction to his encyclical, the Pope reflects on the way water symbolizes the Holy Spirit within the Gospel of John. John reminds us of the promise that Jesus made on the Jewish feast of Tabernacles: "If any one thirst, let him come to me and drink. He who believes in me as the scripture has said, 'Out of his heart shall flow rivers of living water'" (Jn 7:37). The Evangelist himself explains two verses later that Jesus was speaking about the Spirit (see Jn 7:39). The Pope also recalls two of Jesus' numerous conversations—one with a Samaritan woman and another with Nicodemus—in which the Lord used the symbol of water to identify other aspects of the Spirit's character. From the first encounter, John Paul II quotes the Master's words, which ultimately refer to the Spirit, about "a spring of water welling up to eternal life" (Jn 4:14). From the second, he reminds us there is "the need for a new birth 'of water and the Holy Spirit' in order to 'enter the kingdom of God'" (*DV* 1, quoting Jn 3:5).

A new aspect of John Paul II's encyclical about the Holy Spirit as the Giver of Life is a reference to the spiritual heritage of the Oriental Churches. Knowing that the Holy Spirit creates unity, the author indicates a way to Christian unity. He writes on this theme: "In our own age, then, we are called anew by the ever ancient and ever new faith of the Church, to draw near to the Holy Spirit as the giver of life. In this we are helped and stimulated also by the heritage we share with the Oriental Churches, which have jealously guarded the extraordinary riches of the teachings of the Fathers on the Holy Spirit" (*DV* 2).

The power of the Holy Spirit, who gives new life to the Church and through the Church to all people, is also evident by the symbol of fire. As a flame of fire, the Spirit descended on the apostles gathered in the Upper Room and "gave birth" to the Church. A flame of fire over the head of each of Jesus' disciples manifested the presence of the Holy Spirit in them.

John Paul II points to the pivotal role that the Holy Spirit played in the hearts and minds of the apostles. Those who witnessed firsthand "the supreme and most complete revelation of God to humanity [that] is Jesus Christ himself" needed someone else to help them understand what they had seen and pass this knowledge on to others. It was the Holy Spirit who enabled the apostles to communicate this revelation both orally and in writing. Nowadays, "the witness of the Spirit inspires . . . the faithful trans-mission of this revelation (which is contained) in the preaching and writing of the Apostles" (*DV* 5). Without the Holy Spirit, there would have been no testimony of the apostles, and thus, no "human expression [of God's revelation] in the Church and in the history of humanity" (*DV* 5).

Significant renewal took place in the Church after the Second Vatican Council. The Pope underlines, quoting one of the Council's documents, that: "the Spirit dwells in the Church . . . he makes the Church grow, per-petually renews her and leads her to perfect union with her Spouse" (*Lumen Gentium* 4, in *DV* 25).

The Holy Spirit Will Convince the World Concerning Sin, Righteousness, and Judgment

In order to understand properly the role of the Holy Spirit as the one who "will convict the world in regard to sin and righteousness and condemna-tion" (Jn 16:8), we must properly define the terms of this expression, according to John Paul II. Immediately after announcing this particular triple task of the Holy Spirit, Jesus himself gave the following explanation: "in regard to sin, because they do not believe in me; concerning righteous-ness, because I am going to the Father and you will no longer see me; con-demnation, because the ruler of this world has been condemned" (Jn 16:9–11). Sin in this passage "means the rejection of . . . [Jesus'] mission" (*DV* 27), righteousness refers to God the Father restoring to Jesus the "definitive justice" in the glory of heaven, while "? 'judgment' means that the Spirit of truth will show the guilt of the 'world' in condemning Jesus to death on the Cross" (*DV* 27).

The author of the encyclical conveys the truth that only the Holy Spirit can convince us of our sin and lift us up from a moral fall. The Pope states that "convincing" is always God's action, the action of the Holy Spirit, and never the action of a human being, however wise he or she might be.

The Holy Father explains that the "sin against the Holy Spirit" consists in the rejection of the salvific mission of Christ. He says that: "The Holy Spirit, who takes from the Son the work of the Redemption of the world, by this very fact takes the task of the salvific 'convincing of sin.' This convincing is in permanent reference to 'righteousness': that is to say, to definitive salvation in God" (*DV* 28). *Judgment* in this context refers to convincing the world about the guilt of those who condemned Jesus to death on the Cross, because Satan has been judged already and has been defeated; God has emerged victorious.

John Paul II speaks about the role of the Holy Spirit, the Giver of Life, within the redemptive mystery that deals with suffering and death (the "core" of the mystery includes the Resurrection, ascension, and the descent of the Holy Spirit; see *DV* 41).

In view of such a multitude of elevated functions with which the Holy Spirit is entrusted, it might come as a surprise to realize that there appears to be something that the Holy Spirit cannot do, namely, to forgive blasphemy against himself. The Holy Father quotes the relevant passages from the first three Gospels—called the Synoptic Gospels—those of Matthew, Mark and Luke. One ominously sounding quotation will suffice here: "Whoever speaks against the Holy Spirit will not be forgiven" (Mt 12:32).

Thus sin against the Holy Spirit consists in a radical rejection of salvation. The Pope emphasizes that human resistance to the Holy Spirit is the result of the inability to perceive sin. The root causes of this phenomenon today are the falsified images of God and of human beings. A sin of an individual, however, cannot be condoned or absolved by the sin of humanity (such as secular and godless cultures). In today's age, the Pope stresses, there is a great need and loud cry for the Holy Spirit who, while convincing about sin, will convince humanity about salvation. We most desperately need "the intimate action of the Spirit of truth" to safeguard the "integrity of human consciences . . . [and] their healthy sensitivity with regard to good and evil" (*DV* 47).

The Holy Spirit Forms the Conscience

The Pope observes that conscience distinguishes us from other creatures and determines our dignity. After the Vatican Council II's Constitution *Gaudium et Spes* (16), the Holy Father calls our conscience the "most secret core" and our innermost "sanctuary" where we are "alone with God" to listen to his voice (*DV* 43).

The papal encyclical declares the condition of our being "people of conscience" is our cooperation with God and, in particular, our openness to action by the Holy Spirit. The inner conversion of a person and resulting reconciliation with God, neighbor, and self in the sacrament of Penance are fruits of the Holy Spirit. It is because of the Holy Spirit that we are able to remain faithful to God and people, as well as to overcome the temptations of the flesh. There is a constant struggle in our lives between the world of the Spirit and the desires of the flesh. The Pope refers to the words of Saint Paul to the Galatians concerning "the desire of the flesh [are] against the Spirit, and the Spirit against the flesh" (Gal 5:16–17). The Holy Father explains that our constitution of body and spirit does not account for all our inner tensions and contradictions. He contends that "this [internal] struggle . . . belongs to the heritage of sin, is a consequence of sin and at the same time a confirmation of it" (*DV* 55).

We can summarize the Pope's reflection on the words of Saint Paul regarding the inner tensions between spiritual and physical spheres in the following way: human "limitation and sinfulness, which are essential elements of . . . [our] psychological and ethical reality" contrast with God's "giving of divine life in the Holy Spirit." "Who will win?" John Paul II asks, and he answers: "The one who welcomes the gift" (*DV* 55).

Materialism, both practical and theoretical, reveals itself as an external factor contributing to this inner disharmony, according to the Holy Father. But, as the Pope aptly observes: "Materialism is the systematic and logical development of that [internal] resistance and opposition condemned by St. Paul" (*DV* 56). We can speak here of a vicious circle of evil where internal tensions are magnified by external pressures, which had themselves been born from inner divisions of the human heart and mind.

In view of this double danger to human conscience, the internal one arising from original sin, and the external one stemming from materialism and modern moral relativism, the person who wants to retain a pure conscience must remain constantly open to God and the light of the Holy Spirit. The Pope states this very categorically: "Man cannot decide by himself what is good and what is evil . . . [because] God . . . remains the first and sovereign source" (*DV* 36) of this fundamental decision. Being created as we are in God's image and likeness is not only an honor that elevates us above all creatures; it also imposes a duty on us to maintain the clarity of this image by means of our conscience, so that "the image may faithfully reflect its model" (*DV* 36). And it is the Holy Spirit who "gives the gift of conscience" and connects us to the source of the universal moral order in God the Creator. " 'Disobedience' . . . [instead] means the rejection of this source, through man's claim to become an independent and exclusive source for deciding about good and evil" (*DV* 36).

The Holy Spirit and the Time of the Church

The descent of the Holy Spirit upon the apostles gathered in the Upper Room gave rise to the Holy Church. The Church is to be understood in both her human and divine dimensions. God who instituted the Church in the material sphere exists in her until the end of the world; this is the divine dimension of the Church. Jesus called Peter and the apostles to guide the Church on earth. Ever since then, many popes, bishops, and priests have been called. This is the human dimension of the Church. The Church is thus neither purely divine nor exclusively human; she is always both divine and human. Jesus comes to the faithful in the Church by means of the holy sacraments, while the Holy Spirit continues to sanctify the Church and guard infallible divine truth in her. Through the mediation of his Church, God gives all people a chance to meet him. The Pope puts it very succinctly: "Having accomplished the work that the Father had entrusted to the Son on earth (cf. Jn 17:4), on the day of Pentecost the Holy Spirit was sent to sanctify the Church forever, so that believers might have access to the Father through Christ in one Spirit (cf. Eph 2:18)" (*DV* 25).

For centuries, the faithful have been calling to the Holy Spirit for him to renew the face of the earth. The Holy Father feels even greater need to continue this call today and to intensify the urgency of our prayers because "on the horizon of our era there are gathering ever darker 'signs of death': a custom has become widely established . . . of taking the lives of human beings even before they are born, or before they reach the natural point of death" (*DV* 57).

The beneficial changes taking place on earth may be attributable to the Holy Spirit acting in and through us. These changes depend on the authenticity of our deep faith expressed in our way of living. They also depend on our courage to live according to the truth even where the lie prevails. We do change the face of the "big" world around us, that is, the society in which we live, when the Holy Spirit dwells in our "small" world, that is, in our hearts. We act most powerfully when we allow God to act through us. The Pope describes permitting God to work through us as the process of personal maturation: "Man's intimate relationship with God in the Holy Spirit . . . enables him to understand himself, his own humanity, in a new way. . . . Along this path—the path of such an inner maturity . . . —God comes close to man, and permeates more and more completely the whole human world" (*DV* 59).

The Holy Spirit displayed his power to the apostles locked in the Upper Room after the death of Jesus, afraid as they were of persecutions and possible death. When they met the Risen Christ and experienced the loving power of the Holy Spirit the moment he descended upon them, their lives changed radically. They left their hiding place and set forth to spread the Good News of Jesus around the world. The Holy Father described their response to the Spirit in the following words: "With the coming of the Spirit they felt capable of fulfilling the mission entrusted to them. They felt full of strength" (*DV* 25). Yet the Spirit did not limit his activity to the apostles alone. On the contrary, "the grace of the Holy Spirit which the Apostles gave to their collaborators through the imposition of hands continues to be transmitted in Episcopal Ordination" (*DV* 25). The bishops, in their turn, carry on distributing this gift of the Holy Spirit in a twofold manner. When they confer the sacrament of Holy Orders, they "render the sacred ministers sharers in this spiritual gift" (*DV* 25) while in their administration of the sacrament of Confirmation they "ensure that all who are reborn of water and the Holy Spirit are strengthened by this gift." The Pope concludes that in this way "the grace of Pentecost is perpetuated in the Church" (*DV* 25).

The Holy Spirit and Prayer

The Holy Spirit, who lives in the Church and protects her, not only guarantees the infallibility of the Word of God to those who are involved in this activity, but also reveals himself to be an incredibly inspirational and abundant source of creative prayer. Where the breath of the Spirit enters, people gather in numbers to praise God in communal prayer. John Paul II observes that "recent years have been seeing a growth in the number of people who, in ever more widespread movements and groups, are giving first place to prayer and seeking in prayer a renewal of their spiritual life" (*DV* 65).

The Eucharist is for each of us the starting point to other forms of communal or individual prayer. Everyone needs prayer. Others often ask us to pray for them, and the Holy Spirit helps us understand this social dimension of prayer. We live in a world full of noise and impatience, and therefore we need to remember the Holy Father's invitation to be aware of God's presence in our lives. We should consciously and daily create moments of silence for prayer and meditation so as to give ever-deeper meaning to our existence. How eloquent in this context are the words of the liturgical Sequence to the Holy Spirit uttered at the time of Pentecost:

> If you take your grace away
> Nothing pure in men will stay
> All their good is turned to ill.

Pope John Paul II is the model of a man who believes in the power of prayer. The main message of this encyclical about the Holy Spirit is to inform us that the "Holy Spirit is the gift that comes into man's heart together with prayer. . . . He [then] manifests himself . . . as the gift that 'helps us in our weakness' [and when] '. . . we do not know how to pray as we ought . . . the Spirit himself intercedes for us with sighs too deep for words' " (Rom 8:26, in *DV* 65). The Pope is therefore justified in saying: "the Holy Spirit not only enables us to pray, but guides us 'from within' in prayer: he is present in our prayer and gives it a divine dimension" (*DV* 65).

The Holy Father is deeply convinced that a truly prayerful person will necessarily develop a generous attitude toward others after the example of God himself. The formation and manifestation of this openhanded and openhearted attitude became a distinguishing feature his whole papal demeanor and service. He met people from all over the world with open arms; he would greet them joyfully and share with them the gift of his very self. There is no doubt he had learned this attitude in prayer. He knew that God became a gift for us first and continues to come to us as a gift in the Eucharist. Therefore he wrote that it is "especially through the Eucharist, in which man . . . learns to 'find himself . . . through a . . . gift of himself,' . . . [in] communion with God and with others, his brothers and sisters" (*DV* 62, quotation from *Gaudium et Spes* 24).

The Holy Father undertook the task of deepening the mystery of the Holy Spirit in the present encyclical, having entrusted himself totally to the help and power of this Spirit. He always believed in the efficacy of this help and power, and therefore he prayed for the whole of humanity: "Before him I kneel at the end of these considerations, and implore him, as the Spirit of the Father and the Son, to grant to all of us the blessing and grace" (*DV* 67).

6 The Mother of the Redeemer (*Redemptoris Mater*)

March 25, 1987

Introduction

A T THE VERY beginning of his Encyclical *Redemptoris Mater* (*Mother of the Redeemer*), Pope John Paul II highlights the vocation of Mary as well as her deep faith and holiness. He then analyzes the relation of Mary with each of the Persons of the Holy Trinity, and finally emphasizes the role of Mary's motherhood in the development and flourishing of the Church.

The then-approaching two-thousandth anniversary of the birth of the Redeemer provided the Pope with an opportunity to write this encyclical. John Paul II noticed the similarity between the period when Jesus was born (we would call it the original "fullness of time") and our days, and expressed the idea as follows: "when 'the fullness of time' was definitively drawing near—the saving advent of Emmanuel—she who was from eternity destined to be his Mother already existed on earth. The fact that she 'preceded' the coming of Christ is reflected every year in the liturgy of Advent" (*RMat* 3).

The Holy Father intended this encyclical to be an introduction to the Marian Year, which he would proclaim on Pentecost, June 6, 1987, two months following publication of this encyclical. The Pope desired that the faithful deepen their spirituality and faith during the Marian Year by means of her mediation and intercession. We must suppose the Pope wanted all Christians to be distinguished by the same features as Mary. He described the task very clearly: "By means of this Marian Year the Church

53

is called not only to remember everything in her past that testifies to the special maternal cooperation of the Mother of God in the work of salvation in Christ the lord, but also, on her own part, to prepare for the future the paths of this cooperation. For the end of the second Christian Millennium opens up [her cooperative paths] as a new prospect" (*RMat* 49).

New emphasis of the current encyclical is the inclusion of many testimonies of individual people who entrusted their lives to Mary, side-by-side with the usual references to official Church documents, such as the constitutions of the Second Vatican Council or the teachings of earlier popes. John Paul II mentions figures such as Marian devotees Louis Marie Grignion de Montfort and Alfonso Maria de' Liguori.

The Pope, as a highly intellectual person, appreciated all the positive emotional factors of Marian devotion. Referring to the twelfth centenary of the Second Ecumenical Council of Nicaea in 787, John Paul II quotes one of that Council's documents related to popular piety and reminds us that "there could be exposed for the veneration of the faithful, together with the Cross, also images of the Mother of God, of the angels and of the saints, in churches and houses and at the roadside" (*RMat* 33).

In his reflections on Mary's life and her role in the history of salvation, John Paul II compares the Mother of God to a "way" leading to the reconciliation and unity of Christians. He observes with satisfaction that "also among our divided brethren many honor and celebrate the Mother of the Lord, especially among the Orientals. It is a Marian light cast upon ecumenism" (*RMat* 50). The Pope is convinced that true unity of Christians is possible "only if it is based on the unity of their faith" (*RMat* 30). Therefore he urges the faithful to "deepen in themselves and each of their communities that 'obedience of faith' of which Mary is the first and brightest example" (*RMat* 29).

Mary's New Name: "Full of Grace"

John Paul II grounds Mary's exceptional role in the mystery of redemption in her selection by God the Father. The archangel Gabriel confirms this truth at the Annunciation by the way he greets Mary: "Hail, favored one! The Lord is with you" (Lk 1:28). The Pope explains that the angel's intention was for the expression "full of grace" or "favored one" to be taken "as if it were her real name. He does not call her by her proper earthly name:

Miryam [Mary], but by this new name: 'full of grace'" (*RMat* 8). John Paul II proceeds to show the relationship between this new name for Mary and her election from of old and writes: "If the greeting and the name 'full of grace' say all this, in the context of the angel's announcement they refer first of all to the election of Mary as Mother of the Son of God" (*RMat* 9).

In a subsequent reflection, the Pope draws our attention to one of the most essential privileges stemming from Mary's being "full of grace," namely, her Immaculate Conception. The Mother of God revealed her name as the Immaculate Conception during her apparitions at Lourdes. This great truth finds its affirmation in the Bible and in the documents of the Second Vatican Council. John Paul II solemnly declares in his encyclical: "By virtue of the richness of the grace of the beloved Son, by reason of the redemptive merits of him who willed to become her Son, Mary was preserved from the inheritance of original sin" (*RMat* 10). The announcement of the Proto-gospel, as God's promise in Genesis 3:15 is usually called, states: "The seed of the woman [that is, of Mary, the new Eve] will crush the head of the serpent." The serpent symbolizes Satan in the account. Mary is "full of grace," the Holy Father says, "because it is precisely in her that the Incarnation of the Word, the hypostatic union of the Son of God with human nature, is accomplished and fulfilled. As the [Vatican II] Council [Dogmatic Constitution *Lumen Gentium*] says, Mary is 'the Mother of the Son of God. As a result she is also the favorite daughter of the Father and the temple of the Holy Spirit. Because of this gift of sublime grace, she far surpasses all other creatures, both in heaven and on earth'" (*RMat* 9).

Mary's assumption into heaven is mentioned as yet another privilege stemming from her being "full of grace." John Paul II uses the above-mentioned constitution of the Vatican Council and refers to the teaching of Pope Pius XII to reaffirm this truth: "Preserved free from all guilt of original sin, the Immaculate Virgin was taken up body and soul into heavenly glory upon the completion of her earthly sojourn. She was exalted by the Lord as Queen of the Universe, in order that she might be the more thoroughly conformed to her Son, the Lord of lords (cf. Rev 19:16) and the conqueror of sin and death" (*Lumen Gentium*, in *RMat* 41).

Thanks to the divine gift of being "full of grace," Mary intercedes with Almighty God, the disciples of her Son, and her spiritual children on our behalf. We, on the other hand, do not cease to praise her in grateful response. Mary herself expressed this in the words of her Magnificat: "Behold, from now on will all ages call me blessed. The Mighty One has done great things for me, and holy is his name" (Lk 1:48–49).

Mary: The Model of Our Faith

John Paul II repeatedly stresses that Mary merited the title *blessed* through her incredible faith. Mary was greeted with this title by her cousin Elizabeth when the two women met in "the city of Judah," most likely the modern Ain Karim, shortly after the Annunciation. Saint Luke, who described the whole event in his Gospel, underlines that Elizabeth was "filled with the holy Spirit" when she addressed her memorable words to Mary, "Most blessed are you among women, and blessed is the fruit of your womb" (Lk 1:41–42). The Pope remarks that Mary visited her cousin "moved by charity. . . . The reason for her visit is also to be found in the fact that at the Annunciation Gabriel had made special mention of Elizabeth" (*RMat* 12).

The greatness of Mary lies also in the obedience to her faith (see Rom 1:5), as the Pope rightly observes. In spite of the many mysterious statements she heard from the archangel Gabriel at the Annunciation, she responded with her famous words: "Behold, I am the handmaid of the Lord. May it be done to me according to your word" (Lk 1:38). The Pope points out: "This fiat of Mary—'let it be to me'—was decisive, on the human level, for the accomplishment of the divine mystery" (*RMat* 13).

John Paul II compares the faith of Mary to that of Abraham, extols the uniqueness of this virtue in both personages, and highlights the irreplaceable roles the two played in the history of salvation. The Pope concisely states: "In the salvific economy of God's revelation, Abraham's faith constitutes the beginning of the Old Covenant; Mary's faith at the Annunciation inaugurates the New Covenant" (*RMat* 14).

The tremendous strength of Mary's faith was manifested in her reception of the divine mysteries at the moment of Annunciation, and in her acceptance of the many painful experiences related to the life of her Son, as predicted by old Simeon. Mary's trust in God can only be described as "the response to a person's love, and in particular to the love of a mother" (*RMat* 45). John Paul II describes another aspect of this issue in the following words: "To believe means 'to abandon oneself' to the truth of the word of the living God, knowing and humbly recognizing 'how unsearchable are his judgments and how inscrutable his ways' (Rom 11:33). Mary, who by the eternal will of the Most High stands, one may say, at the very center of those 'inscrutable ways' and 'unsearchable judgments' of God, conforms herself to them in the dim light of faith, accepting fully and with a ready heart everything that is decreed in the divine plan" (*RMat* 14).

In his encyclical about Mary, the Mother of the Redeemer, the Pope repeatedly highlights her infinite faith because he wants her to be a model of faith, or rather the model of faith, for all Christ's followers. Steadfast faith and humility are necessary if we are not to lose direction during our earthly pilgrimage. This great desire John Paul II expresses in the following words:

> Let the entire body of the faithful pour forth persevering prayer to the Mother of God and Mother of mankind. Let them implore that she who aided the beginning of the Church by her prayers may now, exalted as she is in heaven above all the saints and angels, intercede with her Son in the fellowship of all the saints. May she do so until all the peoples of the human family, whether they are honored with the name of Christian or whether they still do not know their Savior, are happily gathered together in peace and harmony into the one People of God, for the glory of the Most Holy and Undivided Trinity. (*RMat* 50)

Mary: The Mother of the Church and of All Humanity

The Holy Father John Paul II repeatedly emphasizes that Mary is the Mother of the Church because she was present with the apostles in the Upper Room on the day of Pentecost. The Pope explains that she did not receive the apostolic mission as the apostles did when Jesus sent them to teach all the nations of the world. Instead, she supported the apostles in their mission through her prayers as "the mother of Jesus" (Acts 1:13–14).

The most significant event that fully justifies Mary's titles "Mother of the Church" and "Mother of Humanity" took place at the foot of the Cross on Golgotha. Mary climbed this hill near Jerusalem guided by her faith, fidelity, and love for her Son and for God. When the sacrifice of Jesus was drawing to an end, the Redeemer entrusted Mary to John as mother, and John to Mary as son and disciple. Each one of us, Christ's disciples, becomes a child of Mary, because John symbolically represents each one of us. The Pope includes in its entirety this brief Gospel account of enormous theological value in his encyclical: "Standing by the cross of Jesus were his mother, and his mother's sister, Mary the wife of Clopas, and Mary Magdalene. When Jesus saw his mother, and the disciple whom he loved standing near, he said to his mother: 'Woman, behold your son!' Then he said to the disciple, 'Behold, your mother!' And from that hour the disciple took her to his own home" (Jn 19:25–27, in *RMat* 23).

John Paul II points out that the Second Vatican Council, in line with Tradition, calls Mary " 'the Mother of Christ and mother of mankind': since she 'belongs to the offspring of Adam she is one with all human beings. . . . Indeed she is 'clearly the mother of the members of Christ . . . since she cooperated out of love so that there might be born in the Church the faithful' " (*RMat* 23).

To further justify the import and significance of the title given to Mary, the Pope devotes a number of pages to this issue in the second part of his encyclical, entitled: "The Mother of God at the Center of the Pilgrim Church." He reminds us that all who partake of the spiritual heritage of the Church by this very fact participate in the faith of Mary, the Mother of our Church and our Mother. She believed in God prior to Christ's selection of the apostles, and she strengthens and enlivens the Church ever since. The Pope reflects further and admits that "the Blessed Virgin Mary continues to 'go before' the People of God. Her exceptional pilgrimage of faith represents a constant point of reference for the Church, for individuals and for communities, for peoples and nations and, in a sense, for all humanity" (*RMat* 6).

Following the guidelines of the Second Vatican Council, the Holy Father points to the unique manner in which Mary participated in the life of Jesus, who is the only mediator between God and humanity: only she was involved in this life as the Mother of the Redeemer. In spite of this privileged status, she assumed the role of a servant, calling herself "the handmaid of the Lord" (Lk 1:38) in her conversation with the divine messenger at the Annunciation. She remains a servant, a *handmaid*, of all who are in need of help. Her visit to Elizabeth, who expected a child at the time, proves Mary's concern for human affairs. Her intervention at a wedding in Cana in Galilee when the wine ran short is another example.

Mary, the Mother of the Church and our Mother, remains compassionate, understanding, and extremely sensitive to our needs and requests.

John Paul II describes her presence not only in the life of the ecclesial community but also in the lives of individual believers, concluding that therefore "Mary is honored in the Church 'with special reverence . . . under the title of 'God-bearer.' In all perils and needs, the faithful have fled prayerfully to her protection'" (*RMat* 42).

Mary's Maternal Mediation and Ecumenism

John Paul II, while writing his encyclical on Mary, was fully aware that Mary's role in human redemption is one of the most controversial issues in interdenominational discussions, especially with Protestant churches. In the third part of the document, which deals with the maternal mediation of Mary, he makes direct reference to the Bible, the common foundation of faith for all Christians. In the quoted passage we read that "there is one God, and there is one mediator between God and men, the man Christ Jesus, who gave himself as a ransom for all" (1 Tim 2:5–6, in *RMat* 38).

The Pope honored the presence of the Mother of God in the mystery of Christ and of the Church during the Marian Year. It is worthy of mention that he refers to Tradition, that is the teachings of the Fathers of the Church, to show the place of Mary in the life of the Church in a new light. He writes about it in the following words: "Through the gift . . . of divine motherhood, Mary is united with her Son, the Redeemer, and with his singular graces and offices. By these, the Blessed Virgin is also intimately united with the Church: the Mother of God is a figure of the Church in the matter of faith, charity and perfect union with Christ" (*RMat* 42).

We must be aware that the Holy Father refrains from crediting Mary with the role as a co-redeemer of sins or a dispenser of graces. The Pope states, however, that the Church "throughout her life . . . maintains with the Mother of God a link which embraces . . . the past, the present and the future, and venerates her as the spiritual mother of humanity and the advocate of grace" (*RMat* 47). To be closer to the truth, in another part of his encyclical, he wrote the following words: "Mary's maternal function towards mankind in no way obscures or diminishes the unique mediation of Christ, but rather shows its efficacy. . . . From the text of John it is evident that it is a mediation which is maternal. As the Council proclaims: Mary became 'a mother to us in the order of grace.' This motherhood in the order of grace flows from her divine motherhood. Because she was, by the design of divine Providence, the mother who nourished the divine Redeemer" (*RMat* 22).

Christian unity was very high on Pope John Paul II's agenda. He persistently stressed the need for ecumenical dialogue and was happy to realize that various "Churches and Ecclesial Communities are finding agreement with the Catholic Church on fundamental points of Christian belief, including matters relating to the Virgin Mary" (*RMat* 30). He was particularly optimistic when he wrote about the closeness to the Orthodox Church and the ancient Churches of the East with whom the Catholic Church feels "united by love and praise of the Theotokos [Mother of God]" (*RMat* 31).

John Paul II, while remembering Pope Paul VI's solemn conciliar proclamation of Mary as the Mother of all Christians, passionately urges continuation of all efforts that would "hasten the day when the Church can begin once more to breathe fully with her 'two lungs,' the East and the West" (*RMat* 34).

Mary: A Model of Feminine Dignity

Pope John Paul II could not fail to address contemporary women in his encyclical concerning the one who was "blessed among women" (Lk 1:42). The Pope stresses the need for women to imitate Mary in her humanity in the following words: "It can thus be said that women, by looking to Mary, find in her the secret of living their femininity with dignity and of achieving their own true advancement. In the light of Mary, the Church sees in the face of women the reflection of a beauty which mirrors the loftiest sentiments of which the human heart is capable: the self-offering totality of love; the strength that is capable of bearing the greatest sorrows; limitless fidelity and tireless devotion to work; the ability to combine penetrating intuition with words of support and encouragement." (*RMat* 46).

Another characteristic of Mary upon which John Paul II reflects is her readiness to offer concrete and effective help that goes beyond mere sentimental closeness. This trait of the Mother of Jesus should inspire contemporary women, according to the desires of the Pope. He writes about Mary's "presence in the midst of Israel—a presence so discreet as to pass almost unnoticed by the eyes of her contemporaries—shone very clearly before the Eternal One. . . . With good reason, then . . . we Christians . . . feel the need to emphasize the unique presence of the Mother of Christ in history" (*RMat* 3).

Mary had one more characteristic feature that is important for every spiritually mature person, namely, her ability to listen. She knew how to listen not only to God but to her fellow human beings as well. One day a woman in a crowd shouted to Jesus: "Blessed is the womb that carried you, and the breasts at which you nursed!" (Lk 11:27). The Master agreed that his mother was blessed, but he pointed to a deeper reason for this honor, namely, her ability to "hear the word of God and keep it" (Lk 11:28; see *RMat* 20).

It is important to realize that Mary helps us to grow spiritually and to deepen our union with Jesus through her intercession with God on our behalf. We should imitate her in this respect as well. Those who are concerned with the religious and spiritual development of their fellow human beings, especially mothers caring for their children, display this trait of Mary's very clearly. The Pope is aware of all the evil that occurs in contemporary society in which the little ones must grow, and therefore he points to Mary, who "takes part, as a mother, 'in that monumental struggle against the powers of darkness' which continues throughout human history" (*RMat* 47).

In the conclusion of his encyclical, Pope John Paul II shows Mary as the one who supports all believers in Christ and all people of good will in their daily struggle against calamities and falls.

The Holy Father calls on Jesus, the Redeemer, and on his Blessed Mother to "assist us . . . in the many complicated problems which today beset the lives of individuals, families and nations." He then reassures us regarding the role of Mary that the Church "sees her helping the Christian people in the constant struggle between good and evil, to ensure that it 'does not fall,' or, if it has fallen, that it 'rises again'" (*RMat* 52).

7

On Social Concerns
(*Sollicitudo Rei Socialis*)

December 30, 1987

Introduction

IN HIS SECOND social encyclical, entitled *Sollicitudo Rei Socialis* (*On Social Concerns*), Pope John Paul II morally evaluates the two then-existing sociopolitical blocs known as East and West. He also deals with such issues as peace in the world, poverty in underdeveloped countries, and the potential for full growth for every human being.

The Pope pays equal attention to both rich and poor countries as he reflects on the situation in the contemporary world. He observes "that the frontiers of wealth and poverty intersect within the societies themselves, whether developed or developing. In fact, just as social inequalities down to the level of poverty exist in rich countries, so, in parallel fashion, in the less developed countries one often sees manifestations of selfishness and a flaunting of wealth which is as disconcerting as it is scandalous" (*SRS* 14).

John Paul II sees the principal way to social justice and the just distribution of wealth through spiritual development of each person. This inner growth cumulatively should ultimately lead to the elimination of poverty in all its forms. He is convinced that spiritually mature people will exert positive influences on the economic development of poorer countries and thus contribute to establishment of better human relations. He also reflects on the social doctrine of Pope Paul VI, especially the latter's Encyclical *Populorum Progressio* (*On the Development of Peoples*) and on the documents of the Second Vatican Council. Pope John Paul II employs two important terms when considering human growth—*to be* and *to have*—and elaborates on the differences resulting from the positive focus of being and the negative absorption with wanting to have more. He emphasizes that an amount of accumulated wealth alone does not make a person morally mature or upright because morality and personal maturity depend on each individual's spiritual growth.

John Paul II does not condemn material goods as such; on the contrary, he sees their real potential for good. He believes that material resources create conditions needed not only by an individual to grow as a person, but also by social groups and nations to exist in ever-greater harmony. The Holy Father maintains that the lack of sufficient material resources can even lead to pathologies and social degradation. He says in this regard: "One of the greatest injustices in the contemporary world consists precisely in this: that the ones who possess much are relatively few and those who possess almost nothing are many. It is the injustice of the poor distribution of the goods and services originally intended for all. . . . The evil does not consist in 'having' as such, but in possessing without regard for the quality and the ordered hierarchy of the goods one has. Quality and hierarchy arise from the subordination of goods and their availability to man's 'being' and his true vocation" (*SRS* 28).

The Pope considers participation in the overall process of humanity's development to be an inalienable right of every individual living in every corner of the globe. He solemnly declares that "collaboration in the development of the whole person and of every human being is in fact a duty of all towards all, and must be shared by the four parts of the world: East and West, North and South" (*SRS* 32).

Social Engagement and the Structures of Sin

Pope John Paul II in his search for a way to solve the problem of poverty in the world notes the need to allow every individual the right to undertake his or her own economic initiatives and to grow creatively without restraints. He observes "that the denial of this right, or its limitation in the name of an alleged 'equality' of everyone in society, diminishes, or in practice absolutely destroys the spirit of initiative" (*SRS* 15) The result of this repression or restriction is "passivity, dependence and submission" within society rather than the desired equality of all at a higher level (*SRS* 15).

John Paul II lists other factors that contribute to the increase of poverty in the world, such as total or partial unemployment, the housing crisis, arms trade, the lack of respect for human life, immigration, and international debt.

The Pope is convinced that every type of economic activity carried out by an individual or an organization should be governed by social ethics as well as individual and collective responsibility. He observes that all forms of poverty are mutually interconnected because they are related to the so-called structures of sin. Personal sins, the consequences of original sin, contribute to the creation of whole structures characterized by moral depravation and social injustice. The author reasons: "If the present situation can be attributed to difficulties of various kinds, it is not out of place to speak of 'structures of sin', which . . . are rooted in personal sin, and thus always linked to the concrete acts of individuals who introduce these structures, consolidate them and make them difficult to remove. And thus they grow stronger, spread, and become the source of other sins, and so influence people's behavior" (*SRS* 36).

In order to counter the abovementioned structures of sin, John Paul II recommends holistic individual development, which includes cultural and religious progress, and not merely more materialistic growth geared exclusively toward greater economic output. We find this concern of the Pope in the following words: "Development which is merely economic is incapable of setting man free, on the contrary, it will end by enslaving him further. Development that does not include the cultural, transcendent and religious dimensions of man and society . . . is even less conducive to authentic liberation. Human beings are totally free only when they are completely themselves, in the fullness of their rights and duties. The same can be said about society as a whole" (*SRS* 46).

The Holy Father is convinced that the priority of moral and spiritual values over material goods constitutes a necessary condition for comprehensive personal growth. He argues: "Development . . . must be measured . . . according to . . . [its] interior dimension. . . . On the basis of this teaching, development cannot consist only in the use, dominion over and indiscriminate possession of created things and the products of human industry, but rather in subordinating the possession, dominion and use to man's divine likeness and to his vocation to immortality" (*SRS* 29).

Participation, Solidarity, and the Common Good

John Paul II makes the community aspect of human life into one of the main points of his teachings. We become truly and completely humane through our relations with others. Just as human life has its individual and social dimensions, so also the products of human work have private and corporate characteristics. The author teaches that every person is called to fully committed work for the sake of others: "The obligation to commit oneself to the development of peoples is not just an individual duty, and still less an individualistic one, as if it were possible to achieve this development through the isolated efforts of each individual. . . . In this pursuit of integral human development we can also do much with the members of other religions, as in fact is being done in various places" (*SRS* 32).

The Pope points out that social participation does not consist only in common activities but also in individual activities serving the common good. A mason laying bricks to construct a building's wall can be a good example. The craftsman should be as involved and committed as an engineer or architect who supervises construction of the whole building. The diverse activities and tasks of each worker should complement each other in the realization of a common project for the benefit of all. When workers are treated humanely, their engagement for the common good is called solidarity. The Holy Father expresses this idea in the following words: "The exercise of solidarity within each society is valid when its members recognize one another as persons. Those who are more influential, because they have a greater share of goods and common services, should feel responsible for the weaker and be ready to share with them all they possess. Those who are weaker, for their part, in the same spirit of solidarity, should not adopt a purely passive attitude or one that is destructive of the social fabric, but, while claiming their legitimate rights, should do what they can for the good of all" (*SRS* 39).

Solidarity within particular groups of any society in a given country should serve as a model for other countries in the world, according to the Holy Father. The Pope is convinced that international interdependence should turn to solidarity based on the principle that "the goods of creation are meant for all. That which human industry produces through the processing of raw materials, with the contribution of work, must serve equally for the good of all" (*SRS* 39).

John Paul II sees the way to this local and international solidarity in spirituality, faith, and purity of conscience based on God's law. By means of his encyclical, he invites humanity to deep faith, which is the real foundation of true human solidarity and responsible care for the common good. He challenges us to noble deeds with his description of authentic solidarity: "In the light of faith, solidarity seeks to go beyond itself, to take on the specifically Christian dimensions of total gratuity, forgiveness and reconciliation" (*SRS* 40).

Technical Progress and the Social Question

The Pope—inspired by the contributions of Catholic social teaching—is convinced that social justice should be based on Holy Scripture, that is, on God's revelation. Even a cursory look at human history clearly demonstrates that this has not always been the case. The so-called social question did not arise until the nineteenth century, to give just one example. It was provoked by rapid technical progress, which, however, did not prevent exploitation of workers by factory owners. Now, over a hundred years later, technical progress is even faster, but exploitation of employees still exists, albeit in a markedly different form. John Paul II writes with great concern on this issue: "Given the worldwide dimension which the social question has assumed, this love of the preference for the poor, and the decisions which it inspires in us, cannot but embrace the immense multitudes of the hungry, the needy, the homeless, those without medical care and, above all, those without hope of a better future. It is impossible not to take account of the existence of these realities. To ignore them would mean becoming like the 'rich man' who pretended not to know the beggar Lazarus lying at his gate" (cf. Lk 16:19–31; *SRS* 42).

Since the globalization process does not exclude the spread of injustice from individual countries onto the international scene, John Paul II directs his appeal not only to Christians but to all people of good will. He is not satisfied with mere concern for the poor, or "the Lord's poor" as the Bible poignantly describes them, but demands concrete action on the part of those with power. He urges corrective action in such areas as "the international trade system, which is mortgaged to protectionism and increasing bilateralism; the reform of the world monetary and financial system" (*SRS* 43)—just to name a few.

The Pope calls on all humanity to assume responsibility for the fate of each other, especially the poor and hungry. He proposes to everyone the practice of Christian justice. He criticizes totalitarian systems where human creativity is checked, spiritual values are depreciated, and human dignity is trampled upon. John Paul II highlights with particular force the needs of countries developing at the slowest rate. He is concerned that such countries "instead of becoming autonomous nations concerned with their own progress towards a just sharing in the goods and services meant for all, become parts of a machine, cogs on a gigantic wheel" (*SRS* 22).

Trusting divine providence, which protects the world, the Pope does not lose faith in humanity's moral sense and its instinct for self-preservation (more widespread care for the environment is a sign of this instinct). The Holy Father John Paul II embraces the whole of humanity with his noble thoughts and an open heart and concludes his encyclical with a touching prayer taken from the Roman Missal: "Father, you have given all peoples one common origin, and your will is to gather them as one family in yourself. Fill the hearts of all with the fire of your love, and the desire to ensure justice for all their brothers and sisters. By sharing the good things you give us may we secure justice and equality for every human being, an end to all division and a human society built on love and peace" (*SRS* 49).

8 The Mission of the Redeemer (*Redemptoris Missio*)

December 7, 1990

Introduction

THE FACT THAT the inauguration of Pope John Paul II's pontificate took place on World Mission Day, October 22, 1978, proved to be a prophetic coincidence. The Holy Father turned out to be one of the greatest missionaries of the world. He spread the Good News of Jesus with a total commitment of his heart and mind. His pilgrimages to the remotest corners of the globe ranked among the most efficient methods of contemporary evangelization. Therefore, in his Encyclical *Redemptoris Missio* (*Mission of the Redeemer*), he teaches that faith is born from listening to the Word of God (see Rom 10:17) and is strengthened when shared with others. He made all these journeys for the sake of the gospel. He reminds us that Jesus entrusted the mission of proclaiming the Good News to the apostles when he said: "Go into the whole world and proclaim the gospel to every creature" (Mk 16:15). The Church intuitively understood that these words of Jesus apply to all the baptized. It is not surprising that in this encyclical John Paul II encourages all the faithful, priests and laity alike, to become involved in missionary activity. His main reason for being so emphatic on the issue of the missions is the fact that the kingdom of God has been prepared for all people. The Pope realized that in spite of nearly two thousand years of missionary efforts, the Church has not yet reached the entire population on earth, while the kingdom of God is meant and prepared for everyone. Therefore, he calls with great passion for wholehearted commitment to the proclamation of the gospel. He is very challenging when he states that "this mission [of the Church] is still only [in its] beginning" (*RMiss* 1).

John Paul II is aware that the duty to proclaim the gospel stems from the fact that Jesus Christ is the only Savior, and no one can come to God except through him (see Jn 14:6). The Pope readily admits the existence of "participated forms of mediation of different kinds and degrees" (for example, other religions), but "they acquire meaning and value *only* from Christ's own mediation, and they cannot be understood as parallel or complementary to his" (*RMiss* 5).

The Holy Father analyzes the problems related to the communication of the gospel and divides them into external and internal forms. Among the external challenges, he lists the secular character of our contemporary culture and the falsification of the image of God. The author is convinced, however, that the internal difficulties are more dangerous. The decline of Christian morality, the weakening sense of faith, and the loss of understanding of sin belong to this category. These challenges "must not make us pessimistic or inactive. What counts . . . is the confidence that comes from faith" (*RMiss* 36).

Additionally, this proclamation always happens in a social context, both ecclesial and secular. The breath of the Spirit permeates and molds all these realities because the Spirit is not limited by the visible boundaries of the Church. All peoples, cultures, and religions are affected by the Spirit's activity; the Pope boldly claims that "the Spirit is at the origin of the noble ideals and undertakings which benefit humanity on its journey through history" (*RMiss* 28).

Decisively ecumenical statements as the one above might cause some confusion among the faithful, and therefore John Paul II is careful to distinguish various types of the Holy Spirit's presence. While acknowledging the universal activity of the Spirit, the author points to the Spirit's specific presence and action "within the body of Christ, which is the Church" (*RMiss* 29). The Church welcomes with respect and gratitude all forms of the Spirit's presence in the world, but reserves the right to discern and evaluate them since it was only to the Church that "Christ gave his Spirit in order to guide her into all the truth (cf. Jn 16:13)" (*RMiss* 29).

Evangelization Builds the Kingdom of God

The Pope reminds us in his encyclical that the kingdom of God was the main theme of Jesus' teaching. Jesus' first words in the Gospels of Matthew and Mark are very indicative: "This is the time of fulfillment. The kingdom of God is at hand. Repent, and believe in the gospel" (Mk 1:15; also Mt 4:17). John Paul II remarks that the kingdom of God is an open invitation to all people on the globe, just as is redemption in Christ. It becomes clearer when we realize that under God's reign we learn how "to love, forgive and serve one another"—skills, or rather virtues, that are universally human and not exclusively Christian. The very nature of God's kingdom "is one of communion among all human beings—with one another and with God" (*RMiss* 15). But as Christians, we have a particular duty toward the kingdom. Our working for it means, no more and no less, "acknowledging and promoting God's activity . . . in human history" (*RMiss* 15). And it means removing all forms of evil from our midst because: "the kingdom of God is the manifestation and the realization of God's plan of salvation in all its fullness" (*RMiss* 15).

The idea that God is the sole and proper king of Israel appears prominently in the Old Testament (most dramatically perhaps at the beginning of the monarchy, see especially 1 Sam 8:7), but the term "kingdom of God" appears for the first time on the lips of Jesus (Mk 1:15; Lk 4:43; and as "kingdom of heaven" in Mt 3:2). The Gospel of John uses other symbols to convey the salutary significance of Jesus, but even there the title of "king" frequently applies to Jesus during his ministry (Jn 1:45, 6:15, 12:13), and very poignantly during his Passion, culminating in the placing of an inscription on his Cross which read: "Jesus the Nazorean, the King of the Jews" (Jn 19:19).

This biblical background allows us to appreciate the description of the kingdom of God taken from the Vatican Council II Constitution *Gaudium et Spes* (22), which John Paul II quotes in his encyclical: "The kingdom of God is not a concept, a doctrine, or a program subject to free interpretation, but it is before all else *a person* with the face and name of Jesus of Nazareth, the image of the invisible God." The Pope warns against two dangerous trends in the interpretation of the kingdom of God. In one case, the kingdom tends to be separated from the person of Jesus and is thus reduced to "a purely human or ideological goal" (*RMiss* 18) where

Christ's true identity suffers. In the other trend, the kingdom of God is separated from the Church, which is after all "the seed, sign and instrument" (*RMiss* 18) of this kingdom. While it is true that we cannot exclusively identify the Church with Christ or his kingdom, we cannot deny either that the Church is the body of Christ, which is sanctified by the Holy Spirit. We are "not excluding the action of Christ and the Spirit outside the Church's visible boundaries" here, but merely affirming "the Church's special connection with the kingdom of God and of Christ," and her "mission of announcing and inaugurating [it] among all peoples" (*RMiss* 18; last phrase quoted from *Lumen Gentium* 5).

To conclude our reflection on the relationship between evangelization and the kingdom of God as delineated by John Paul II in his encyclical, we should also realize the connection between this kingdom and salvation. The Pope says that the kingdom of God comes to its perfection and completion when we accept "the mystery of the Father and of his love, made manifest and freely given in Jesus through the Spirit," and this is precisely what salvation is. The Church has only to work and pray "for its perfect and definitive realization" (*RMiss* 12).

The Holy Spirit and the Missionary Character of the Church

The Holy Spirit has been revealed as the fruit of love from the Father and Son. He is also the source of love and life of the Church, since he is the one who has been guiding the Church along missionary paths since the day of Pentecost. He should truly and properly be called "the principal agent of the whole of the Church's mission" (*RMiss* 21), and especially so of the mission directed to the nations.

The Pope underlines that the Church has always had a missionary character. Even before she was officially instituted on the day of Pentecost, Jesus had announced that his disciples would be sent "to the ends of the earth" (Acts 1:8). They were never to be alone on this mission. John Paul II states that all the so-called "missionary mandates" in the Synoptic Gospels and in the Acts of the Apostles contain the assurance that Jesus through the Holy Spirit would accompany the disciples. The command of the Risen Lord remains in force, while the promise continues to encourage all believers to engage in missionary activity. Jesus was, namely, the supreme missionary of the Father, and we as his followers are called to imitate our Master and Savior. The Pope reminds us of Jesus' statement regarding his own mission: "As the Father has sent me, so I send you" (Jn 20:21). Jesus indeed has sent the Church on her mission; therefore she is missionary by her very nature, and not merely by the fact that some of her members are sent to the missions. As the Pope aptly puts it: "we are missionaries above all because of *what we are* as a Church . . . even before we become missionaries *in word or deed*" (*RMiss* 23).

The Holy Father reminds all missionaries—clerics and lay people alike—of the presence of the Holy Spirit not only in themselves but also in those who are receiving the gospel through them. Special as the presence of the Spirit in the Church most definitely is, we must not forget about the "seeds of the Word" outside the visible structures of the Church. The Second Vatican Council used this descriptive phrase to acknowledge the presence of the Holy Spirit in the lives of those who do not recognize Jesus as their Lord and Savior. The Pope uses even stronger language to describe the universal presence of the Holy Spirit when he analyzes one of the conciliar documents: "We are obliged to hold that the Holy Spirit offers everyone the possibility of sharing in the Paschal Mystery in a manner known to God" (*RMiss* 6). Moreover, "The Spirit offers the human race 'the light and strength to respond to its highest calling'" (*RMiss* 28). And it is not a question of some emergency intervention: "The Spirit . . . is at the very source of man's existential and religious questioning . . . which is occasioned . . . by the very structure of his being" (*RMiss* 28, quotations from *Gaudium et Spes* 22 and 10).

Experiences of those who take part in interreligious prayers and meetings could serve as a good illustration of the Pope's thesis about the universal presence of the Spirit. Denying this presence and activity would not only mean lack of "respect for man in his quest for answers to the deepest questions of his life," but even more ominously, not to say blasphemously, lack of "respect for the action of the Spirit in man" (*RMiss* 29) Ultimately, and John Paul II is absolutely convinced about it, "every authentic prayer is prompted by the Holy Spirit, who is mysteriously present in every human heart" (*RMiss* 29).

The Pope takes stock of the history of the missions in his encyclical as well. Past experiences should motivate us today in continuing to express the universal character of the Church as well as her missionary character. In this spirit of grateful recognition, the Pope lists a number of anniversaries that had either taken place shortly before he issued the current encyclical or were to follow soon after, such as the millennium of the evangelization of Russia and the Slav peoples, the five hundredth anniversary of the evangelization of the Americas, and the centenaries of the first missions in various countries of Asia, Africa, and Oceania (see *RMiss* 30).

The Pope admits that today the Church faces new challenges in her journey through history. The imperative to proclaim Christ remains paramount, however, especially so if we remember that two-thirds of humanity do not yet recognize Jesus as their Savior. Our ardent faith and authentic lives are vital if this situation is to change. A look at the past can help, and therefore the Pope appeals to "all Christians, the particular churches and the universal Church . . . to have the same courage that inspired the missionaries of the past, and the same readiness to listen to the voice of the Spirit" (*RMiss* 30).

Dimensions of Evangelizing Activity

The missionary activity of the Church does not take place in a vacuum. The incredible speed with which the contemporary world has been changing creates a specific challenge for the Church, which strives to carry out the mandate received from Christ nearly two thousand years ago. Some of these changes are predominantly secular in nature, like rapid urbanization and economical or political migration. Other changes belong to the sphere of religion and culture. The Pope mentions "the de-Christianization of countries with ancient Christian traditions," but notes the apparently contradictory tendency of "the increasing influence of the Gospel and its values in overwhelmingly non-Christian countries, . . . [while] the proliferation of messianic cults and religious sects" reminds us about the hunger for spiritual food of the contemporary human being (*RMiss* 32).

In spite of the fact that evangelization can be understood in various ways, the Holy Father is convinced that the mission *ad gentes*, that is, the mission addressed to those who have not yet known Christ, remains a valid and binding obligation of the Church, since it has not been completed. This is missionary activity properly so-called, but certainly not the only situation where the Church needs to focus her evangelizing attention.

The gospel needs to be proclaimed not only to those who have not yet heard about it but also to those who live by its values on a daily basis. Those Christians who have formed well-organized communities, who have structured their lives according to the message of Jesus, and who give testimony of their faith in the societies where they live call for continued evangelization as well. The response of the Church to this demand is usually called pastoral care.

The third and final situation where evangelization takes place is among those baptized Christians or Christian societies who have lost their commitment of faith or even their Christian identity. They cannot be called pagan anymore, but it is questionable whether to consider them Christian, especially because they often do not acknowledge their belonging to any Church. Here the Pope sees the need for a "new evangelization" or a "re-evangelization" (see *RMiss* 33).

Helpful as this classification might be, John Paul II warns that "the boundaries between *pastoral care of the faithful, new evangelization* and *specific missionary activity* are not clearly definable, and it is unthinkable to create barriers between them or to put them into watertight compartments" (*RMiss* 34).

The abovementioned three different situations where the Church proclaims the gospel gave rise to some confusion in the way we speak about the missions. Ecumenical openness of the Church toward other religions after the Second Vatican Council (1962–1965) complicated the picture even further. Some began to question whether it still made sense to spread the gospel of Jesus if the Spirit were present outside the visible structures of the Church, and if salvation were possible to those who were not baptized in the name of Jesus. The term *evangelization* (from the Greek *euangelion*, meaning "good news") gradually replaced *mission* (from the Latin *mission*, meaning "sending") in some quarters. In this context, the Pope strongly reiterates the need for revitalized evangelization along with enhanced missionary activity: "Saying that all Catholics must be missionaries . . . requires that there be persons who have a specific vocation to be life-long missionaries *ad gentes*" (*RMiss* 32).

John Paul II understood well the difficulties the Church faces in carrying out her mission of spreading the faith in today's world, and therefore he entrusted to Mary's mediation not just the Church in general but those committed to fulfilling this missionary mandate in particular. "As Christ sent forth his apostles . . . so too, renewing that same mandate, I extend to all of you my apostolic blessing" (*RMiss* 92).

The Role of Lay People in Evangelization

John Paul II teaches in his encyclical that lay people are called to be fully involved in the evangelization process on the basis of their baptism, and when they do so, they merit the title of missionaries. They enjoy a certain advantage over the clergy in that they live among other lay people for whom they can be daily witnesses of the gospel. The testimony of a Christian life is, namely, the first and the most basic form of spreading the faith, as the Holy Father readily admits. It has always been the case but has become even more important in this age of omnipresent advertising and enticing promotions. He accurately observes: "People today put more trust in witnesses than in teachers, in experience than in teaching, and in life and action than in theories" (*RMiss* 42).

Since Jesus Christ is the ultimate subject of the Church's proclamation, all Christians who want to fulfill their missionary task even as witnesses—not to mention those who choose to spread the Good News *ad gentes* (that is, to the nations)—must welcome Christ in his totality into their lives. They cannot proclaim their own version of Christ, even if his grace is unique for every one of them. It is the Christ of the Creed that the Christians must proclaim, the one who was crucified, died, and has risen. Only "through him is accomplished our full and authentic liberation from evil, sin and death; through him God bestows 'new life' that is divine and eternal." We do not have any other message for the world but the word of Christ, "which changes man and his history, and which all peoples have a right to hear" (*RMiss* 44).

The gospel proclaimed by the Church changes the world in more ways than one. Missionaries, especially the laity, who are often professionals in such fields as engineering or medicine, are frequently recognized more as "promoters of development" than evangelizers. While it is true that the Good News of Christ offers a comprehensive human growth, it does so from within, and not exclusively by means of technical or educational assistance. Schools, hospitals, and printing presses do help but cannot replace the proclamation of the gospel message. The principal task of the Church is to reveal "to peoples the God whom they seek and do not yet know." The Church does so by revealing "the grandeur of man created in God's image and loved by him, the equality of all men and women as God's sons and daughters . . . [but also] the obligation to work for the development of the whole person and of all mankind" (*RMiss* 58).

The Holy Father describes numerous ways in which lay people can become involved in the process of evangelization. They can do so outside the structures of the Church, and this is the field proper to them. Politics as well as social and economic spheres of life are domains where the laity should plant "the seeds of the Word" by means of the witness of their lives. The laity has also a great role to play within the Church, and the Pope is happy to mention? "the rapid growth of 'ecclesial movements' filled with missionary dynamism" in many local churches. At their best, "these movements . . . represent a true gift of God both for new evangelization and for missionary activity" (*RMiss* 72).

Love for neighbor and love for truth are to characterize every missionary as well, according to the Pope. Missionary activity without these attributes is impossible. A missionary, whether lay or ordained, should always serve the truth. Since we are all called to be missionaries, "we must ponder the mysterious ways of the Spirit and allow ourselves to be led by him into all the truth (cf. Jn 16:13)" (*RMiss* 87). When it comes to love for neighbor, the Holy Father quotes a document of Latin American bishops who spoke about the poor, but their words can be applied to all who receive the missionary proclamation: "The poor deserve preferential attention, whatever their moral or personal situation. They have been made in the image and likeness of God to be His children, but this image has been obscured and even violated. For this reason, God has become their defender and loves them . . . and their evangelization is . . . the sign and proof of the mission of Jesus" (*RMiss* 60).

Courage in Proclaiming the Gospel

John Paul II reflects on a Greek word *parrhesia* (literally "boldness," "enthusiasm" or "energy"), in order to highlight the need for courage in proclaiming the gospel. The word appears frequently in the Acts of the Apostles, and Saint Paul describes his own attitude with this term: "We drew courage in our God to declare to you the Gospel of God in the face of great opposition" (1 Thes 2:2, in *RMiss* 45). And Saint Paul was not exaggerating when he spoke about "much struggle." He faced opposition not just from Gentiles or Jews but from false brothers as well. He was flogged, stoned, and shipwrecked, all for the sake of the gospel. To add to those difficulties, he was also under daily pressure because of his anxiety for all the churches (see 2 Cor 11:24–28), in places of frequent tensions, amidst quarrels and divisions. He, as well as the other apostles, faced all these obstacles with courage, with *parrhesia*, the quality the Pope wants all contemporary missionaries to have.

The attitude of Peter and John in front of the council of Jewish elders and priests can also serve as a good illustration of this newly found strength and courage. Faced with the order to stop proclaiming the Resurrection of Jesus, the two replied: "It is impossible for us not to speak about what we have seen and heard" (Acts 4:20).

The author clearly indicates in his encyclical that the source of Christian courage is Christ himself. In order to give us strength and instill in us the gift of Christian courage, the Holy Father recalls the words of Saint Paul to the Romans: "For I am not ashamed of the gospel. It is the power of God for the salvation of everyone who believes" (Rom 1:16). This spiritual power of God emboldened all Christian martyrs who gave their lives for Christ.

John Paul II refers to Mary, the Mother of our Savior, in almost all of his encyclicals. He wants her to be always present in the Church, just as she was with the apostles in the Upper Room after the ascension of Christ. For this to happen, the Pope invites the Church, spread as she is around the world, to "gather in the Upper Room 'together with Mary, the Mother of Jesus' (Acts 1:14), in order to pray for the Spirit and to gain strength and courage to carry out the missionary mandate" (*RMiss* 92). We, the missionaries of Christ in the world of today, just like the apostles and the missionaries of the past, "need to be transformed and guided by the Spirit" (*RMiss* 92).

Evangelization in a New Culture

Jesus Christ is the object of the evangelizing activity of the Church, and the only proper recipient of Jesus Christ is a human being. Therefore, we can speak of the evangelization of culture and of the mass media only in metaphorical, nontechnical terms. And this is what the Holy Father does in his Encyclical *Redemptoris Missio*. He speaks of the need to infuse the values of the gospel into the mass media and into cultures because those two products of human creativity heavily influence their users. In turn, they are simply too powerful to be ignored if Christ's message is to reach "to the ends of the earth" (Acts 1:8).

John Paul II sees the need to focus the attention of the Church on the mass media, something that has often been neglected in the past. This may not have been possible previously, but the mass media today, not simply an expression of culture (if they had ever been only that), form an integral part of it, and we now find they mandate our attention. "In particular, the younger generation is growing up in a world conditioned by the mass media," the Pope writes. The influence of the world of communications is so powerful that the world is being turned into a "global village." The Pope's analysis of this phenomenon is both helpful and challenging at the same time: "Since the very evangelization of modern culture depends to a great extent on the influence of the media, it is not enough to use the media simply to spread the Christian message. . . . It is also necessary to integrate that message into the 'new culture' created by modern communications" (*RMiss* 37). John Paul II, referring to Saint Paul's speech in the Areopagus in Athens during one of his missionary trips (see Acts 17:19–34), calls the mass media "the first Areopagus of the modern age" (*RMiss* 37).

The Pope reflects on the way the gospel enters a particular culture in the process usually called inculturation. This process is important for all Christians since they all live in a culture that needs to be constantly challenged by the gospel, however Christian it might call itself. But it is of paramount importance for the missionaries who proclaim the gospel in cultures that have not been touched by evangelical values. A missionary from Europe, for example, must remember to proclaim the Christ of the gospel in Africa or Asia, and not the supposedly Christian culture of the old continent. Inculturation properly understood does not destroy what is good in a local culture, but assumes all its positive values in order to elevate them by means of the gospel. Dance, an integral part of African culture, can carry a deep religious message even during the Eucharist. All those involved in the issues of mission in the service of the gospel should be patient and responsible. John Paul II writes that

the process of the Church's insertion into peoples' cultures is a lengthy one. It is not a matter of purely external adaptation, for inculturation "means the intimate transformation of authentic cultural values through their integration in Christianity and the insertion of Christianity in the various human cultures" (Extraordinary Assembly of 1985, Final Report, II, D, 4). . . . Through inculturation the Church makes the Gospel incarnate in different cultures and at the same time introduces peoples, together with their cultures, into her own community (Apostolic Exhortation *Catechesi Tradendae*, 53). She transmits to them her own values, at the same time taking the good elements that already exist in them and renewing them from within (Paul VI, Apostolic Exhortation *Evangelii Nuntiandi*, 20). (*RM* 52)

Patience during the whole process is absolutely necessary since superficial adaptation is simply not enough. And it is not just the culture that is changing in the process of evangelization—the Church is changing too. The universal Church becomes richer when one of her parts makes a positive contribution for the benefit of all: "She comes to know and to express better the mystery of Christ, all the while being motivated to continual renewal," as the Holy Father puts it (*RMiss* 52). This renewal is to be guided by a dual principle of "compatibility with the gospel and communion with the universal Church" (*RMiss* 54, quoting the 1981 Apostolic Exhortation *Familiaris Consortio*).

John Paul II lists other areas that need to be covered by the evangelizing activity of the Church. He mentions engagement for the promotion of peace, the development of peoples, individual human rights and the rights of nations, defense of the rights of women and children, as well as protection of the environment. The Holy Father wants the gospel to shed its light on scientific research and on the debates dealing with international relations. All these areas, and others, must be covered so that the mission of the Redeemer, *Redemptoris Missio*, can continue to bear abundant fruit for the sake of all humanity.

9

The Hundredth Year
(*Centesimus Annus*)

May 1, 1991

Introduction

THE THIRD social encyclical of John Paul II, *Centesimus Annus* of 1991, was occasioned by two important historical events: the centenary of the first social encyclical by Leo XIII of 1891 (thus the title, *The Hundredth Year*) and the fall of communism in eastern and central Europe in 1989.

John Paul II reminds us that it was the Church that showed nineteenth-century capitalism a way of reform, most especially in *Rerum Novarum*. Leo XIII (in his 1891 encyclical) opposed nationalizing the means of production. He defended the dignity of workers and their right to free engagement in economic activities. He did not want the worker to be a mere cog in a state machine. His encyclical also included abolishing the disproportion of wealth between poor and rich, the guarantee of just wages and security of employment for workers, as well as social security for the unemployed.

John Paul II identifies the objectification of a person and the violation of human rights as key reasons for the fall of Marxist communism behind the "iron curtain." This system not only takes away human dignity but also attempts to fill the hearts of citizens with the spiritual void of atheism. The Holy Father emphasizes that the demise of communism in 1989 should be seen as a victory by workers, and of those who live by gospel values. The Pope reckons this event of universal importance as "a warning to those who, in the name of political realism, wish to banish law and morality from the political arena" (*CA* 25).

Apart from the two significant events mentioned above, John Paul II also highlights new elements in the social teaching of the Church. The Pope appreciates the free market system and democracy provided by capitalism, but points to their limitations and the danger of distortions. He upholds the principle of subsidiarity in relations between society and the state. John Paul II is convinced that the state should interfere in affairs of smaller societies within it only when they are not self-sufficient. In this way, the nature of a society as a subject independent from the state would be safeguarded. John Paul II accentuates the importance of culture in human life and rates it above economy and politics in the hierarchy of human needs. Because social life is governed by ethical laws, society needs the Church as a custodian defining what is right and wrong, according to the Pope. It is especially noteworthy that the author of the encyclical makes a crucial distinction between faith and ideology.

The Pope writes also about the need for truth and honesty in any economic activity, and the necessity of treating a human being personally. These values should form the foundations of any democracy. He deals with goods common to the whole of society, such as the environment, that need to be protected. He states that an individual should not selfishly get rich at the expense of others. Considering the world economic situation at the time, he points to the need of applying ethical norms in economic life not only at the level of an individual, but also in the life of a nation, and on a global scale as well.

Ethics of a Free Market

John Paul II sees capitalism as a new social and economic order because it appreciates human creativity, as opposed to communism, which does not. This is the reason why he expresses his support for a market economy in *Centesimus Annus*. He is convinced that a free market best provides for basic human needs, better utilizes natural resources, while facilitating the exchange of goods at the same time. Immediately after highlighting the positive aspects of a free market economy, he warns against idealizing it. He stresses forcefully the need to focus first on a human being with his or her moral values before paying attention to any material gain in free-market transactions. He believes that working people have the right to strive for full respect of their human dignity and to acquire broader access to co-ownership of the means of production. Referring to his first social encyclical, *Laborem Exercens*, the Pope negatively evaluates any economic system that upholds "the absolute predominance of capital, the possession of the means of production and of the land, in contrast to the free and personal nature of human work" (*CA* 35).

The Holy Father also believes that the respect shown to workers leads to greater productivity and efficacy in their work. When workers are treated as co-owners, they have a sense that their work not only provides for their personal needs and the needs of their families, but also serves their local community, nation, and humanity as a whole. He expresses this idea in the following words: "The integral development of the human person through work does not impede but rather promotes the greater productivity and efficiency of work itself. . . . Each person collaborates in the work of others and for their good" (*CA* 43).

John Paul II expresses the conviction that the free market will not solve the problems of social justice in the contemporary world, especially that of hunger in poor countries. Therefore, referring to the Catholic social teaching of his predecessors, especially of Leo XIII, he deals with the issue of common use of goods in his Encyclical *Centesimus Annus*. He reminds us that God is the first and fundamental good for a human being. God created both humanity and the earth, so that by tilling the ground people might find their sustenance (see Gen 1:29). Everybody, and not just the rich, have the right to land. This is the reason why the Vicar of Christ teaches the need for cooperation between rich and poor countries when it comes to accessing earth's resources. He reminds us that the citizens of all countries should be aware that created goods are meant for everybody.

The Holy Father draws our attention to the need to share the fruits of our labor with others. He recalls that at the beginnings of human society tilling the ground was the main source of income. Now, income comes from the products of human work. In view of this, the Pope emphasizes that "besides the earth, man's principal resource is *man himself*" (*CA* 32). Writing about the contemporary situation, the Holy Father considers knowledge and the products of human work, such as sophisticated technology, as property. The prosperity of the industrialized countries is based on property developed by human work and not just on natural resources. Just like the earth, this modern type of property has a common destination and use. The author indicates the need for sharing the achievements of contemporary technological progress between rich and poor countries. Calling for the reawakening of consciences, he shows in his encyclical the existence of "the human inadequacies of capitalism and the resulting domination of things over people" (*CA* 33).

Protection of Natural and Human Environment

John Paul II makes us aware that the purity of the natural and human environment is always linked to the maturity and responsibility of the individual. He admits with sadness, however, that some people use the earth's resources in a disorderly manner because they are guided solely by their desire to possess. Blinded by their craving for profit, they become arbitrary masters of the earth, destroying in the process both the natural habitat as well as the moral environment of other people. They exploit the earth as if they were convinced that its resources were unlimited. The consequences of this behavior are the destruction of nature, the pollution of air and water, as well as accompanying deterioration to human health. The Holy Father reminds us that everybody has the right to clean air and water and to have respect for their habitat, that is, including their spiritual, intellectual, and emotional integrity. God's command to subdue the earth (see Gen 1:28) calls us to cooperate with God in respecting life.

The Pope observes that an arbitrary attitude toward the natural environment contributes to its destruction: "Man thinks that he can make arbitrary use of the earth, subjecting it without restraint to his will, as though it did not have its own requisites and a prior God-given purpose, which man can indeed develop but must not betray" (*CA* 37). He evaluates the attitude described in this quotation in terms of spiritual poverty and mediocrity, which point to an egoistic desire to possess. For many people, this obsessive drive to possess ranks higher than the pristine beauty of nature, which constitutes a common heritage for present and future generations.

The author emphasizes that apart from the senseless destruction of our natural environment we also witness nowadays "the more serious destruction of the *human environment*" with "too little effort . . . made to *safeguard the moral conditions for an authentic 'human ecology'*" (*CA* 38). He teaches us that it is not only the earth that has been given to us by God so that we take care of it, but also our own humanity. This is the reason why everyone should respect our natural human dignity and moral sensitivity. It is particularly important that every person, especially our youth, have morally healthy family, school, and neighborhood environments. John Paul II (echoing Pius XI's Encyclical *Quadragesimo Anno*) calls us boldly to oppose demoralized societies and the so-called "structures of sin" in which we live. He writes about it in the following words: "To destroy such structures and replace them with more authentic forms of living in community is a task which demands courage and patience" (*CA* 38).

Having healthy moral development for individuals in mind, the Pope underlines that the first and basic cell of "human ecology" is the family. Parents who love and respect each other create a morally healthy environment for their children; thus the offspring will find it easier to love and respect other people in turn. This is the reason why he urges us "to go back to seeing the family as the *sanctuary of life* . . . it is the place in which life—the gift of God—can be properly welcomed and protected against the many attacks to which it is exposed. . . . In the face of the so-called culture of death, the family is the heart of the culture of life" (*CA* 39).

Participation or Alienation?

John Paul II evaluates two economic systems, communism and capitalism, from the point of view of human participation in economic activity, that is, in work and in the production of goods. He reminds us that the Marxists criticized capitalism for alienating people by reducing them to the role of a commodity. He states that the communist accusation is based on a false concept of alienation, which is reduced to the spheres of production and property alone. The Holy Father remarks that communism not only did not eliminate alienation but, on the contrary, increased it by the fact that people lacked things necessary for living, which led to ultimate economic collapse.

The false communist diagnosis of alienation in the capitalist system not withstanding, the very historical experience of the West demonstrates the existence of social alienation of people in this system as well, the Pope points out. In spite of his negative attitude toward communism and some aspects of capitalism, John Paul II does not propose the so-called "third way" as an ideal system either. Referring to the Vatican II Constitution *Gaudium et Spes* and Paul VI's Apostolic Letter *Octogesima Adveniens*, he writes: "The Church has no models to present; models that are real and truly effective can only arise within the framework of different historical situations, through the efforts of all those who responsibly confront concrete problems in all their social, economic, political and cultural aspects, as these interact with one another" (*CA* 43).

John Paul II underlines that human alienation in capitalism has its root in the fact that people often acquire the means necessary for living in the spirit of consumerism while neglecting the development of their personality. He sees the reason for alienation at work in the lack of full self-realization of an employee. This happens when the employer is geared solely to maximizing profit regardless of the worker's personal and social situation. The Pope writes that the degree of human alienation or participation depends on the way workers are treated—either as tools necessary to achieve an economic goal, or as members of an authentic community of workers who are valuable as people.

Promulgating the Christian vision of the human being in his Encyclical *Centesimus Annus*, the author describes two ways of thinking. The first treats human life as a vocation with a mission to accomplish, while the second refers only to a sum of feelings that needs to be experienced. People who do not respect values and their own grandeur as persons, or do not respect others, deprive themselves of the possibility of living fully their own humanity. They do not establish relationships with others based on solidarity, something for which they were primarily created by God. John Paul II remarks that people become truly human and capable of participating in the lives of others when they discover a reference to God in their behavior. He echoes *Gaudium et Spes* (41), which grounds the meaning of man's existence in his relationship to God: "Man cannot give himself to a purely human plan for reality, to an abstract ideal or to a false utopia. As a person, he can give himself to another person or to other persons, and ultimately to God, who is the author of his being and who alone can fully accept his gift" (*CA* 41).

Society and State

When dealing with the problem of "the state" in his Encyclical *Centesimus Annus*, the author points to two dimensions of the issue: the first treats a state in relation to other states (external), while the second looks at the internal relations within a given state. Just as the prosperity of an individual is dependent on other people, so it is among nations, where the same logic applies. The Pope states that "recent experience has shown that countries which [isolate themselves] . . . have suffered stagnation and recession, while the countries which experienced development were those which succeeded in taking part in the general interrelated economic activities at the international level" (*CA* 33).

The Holy Father reminds us that the state is a structure meant to help individuals and society achieve individual and social goals. This cannot happen in a totalitarian state, where individuals or groups of people do not have meaning nor value of their own but are always subordinated to state ideology. The position of people in a democratic state is radically different, in that they have control over their own lives.

The role of the state in the economic sphere, the Pope emphasizes, is to guarantee its citizens a sense of security when it comes to freedom and property, as well as to secure the stability of its currency and efficient functioning of public services. Creating favorable conditions for the development of education, culture, and social security, as well as the protection of the environment, are also tasks of the state. A so-called welfare state (Social Assistance State) emerged in the twentieth century. It is characterized by the far-reaching intervention of the state into the lives of individuals and social groups within it. Although John Paul II sees the need for the existence of a state as such, he favors the limitation of its role, and strongly rejects the idea of a welfare state because: "the Social Assistance State leads to a loss of human energies and an inordinate increase of public agencies, which are dominated more by bureaucratic ways of thinking than by concern for serving their clients" (*CA* 48).

The Holy Father explains that the state is not the only institution responsible for social assistance and education. He reminds us that the Church has been meeting the needs of people for centuries. In order to carry out her function as a social assistance agent, the Church appeals to families (as just one instance) to take care of the elderly, and not deprive them of human feelings by sending them to homes for the aged. The Church guards human dignity from the moment of conception until natural death. Therefore, he calls for unity in the family because it protects human dignity and creates a positive educational model.

The author of the encyclical also points out that the role of a democratic state is to guarantee its citizens free access to the truth, that is, to true freedom, where moral values of individuals and of society are its essential content. He expresses this idea in the following way:

> Authentic democracy is possible only in a State ruled by law, and on the basis of a correct conception of the human person. It requires that the necessary conditions be present for the advancement both of the individual through education and formation in true ideals, and of the "subjectivity" of society through the creation of structures of participation and shared responsibility. . . . But freedom attains its full development only by accepting the truth. In a world without truth, freedom loses its foundation and man is exposed to the violence of passion and to manipulation, both open and hidden. (*CA* 46)

The Principle of Subsidiarity and the Common Good

One of the key ideas of John Paul II presented in *Centesimus Annus* is the service of the state toward society. He explains that when we talk about a society, we have in mind a community of human beings and their individual activities. In this way, the nature of a society as a unit is expressed. The state should interfere in the lives of individual societies only when needed, when they are no longer self-sufficient. This intervention is what we call the principle of subsidiarity. Recalling Pius XI's Encyclical *Quadragesimo Anno*, he defines this principle as follows: "A community of a higher order should not interfere in the internal life of a community of a lower order, depriving the latter of its functions, but rather should support it in case of need and help to coordinate its activity with the activities of the rest of society, always with a view to the common good" (*CA* 48).

The Pope warns individual countries against excessive growth of its administration, which always functions at the expense of human needs. He emphasizes, as did Leo XIII in his Encyclical *Rerum Novarum*, that the individual, family, and society are more important than administrative structures, and therefore "the State exists in order to protect their rights and not stifle them" (*CA* 11).

Centesimus Annus also indicates that the role of the state is to take care of the common good for society. One of the key manifestations of this care is the guarantee of human rights to all citizens. The rights to life, truth, freedom, work, medical care, and growth belong in this category. Another important manifestation of common good that is crucial for human growth is culture. Pope John Paul II, who grew up in an atmosphere where human culture and especially Christian culture were being destroyed, points to the dangers that culture may face from the state: "The culture and praxis of totalitarianism also involve a rejection of the Church. The State or the party which claims to be able to lead history towards perfect goodness, and which sets itself above all values, cannot tolerate the affirmation of an *objective criterion of good and evil.* . . . Furthermore, the totalitarian State tends to absorb within itself the nation, society, the family, religious groups and individuals themselves" (*CA* 45).

The Pope knows that human beings are the source and creators of culture in its many forms, and this is the reason why he encourages everyone to participate in its development. Especially significant are his words about culture in general, and about spiritual culture in particular: "Man is understood in a more complete way when he is situated within the sphere of culture through his language, history, and the position he takes towards the fundamental events of life, such as birth, love, work and death. At the heart of every culture lies the attitude man takes to . . . the mystery of God" (*CA* 24).

10 The Splendor of Truth (*Veritatis Splendor*)

August 6, 1993

Introduction

POPE JOHN PAUL II begins his Encyclical *Veritatis Splendor* (*The Splendor of Truth*) with his conviction that the splendor of truth shines in all the works of God, and most especially in each human being, who has been created in his image and likeness (see Gen 1:26). Many people influenced by contemporary culture live "as if God did not exist" (*VS* 88) in spite of the enormous bank of scientific knowledge that should point everyone toward the existence of a Creator. In his encyclical, the Holy Father focuses on the teaching of the Church regarding Christian morality. He unequivocally points out that God's law is the source of morality. A person enlightened by God should come to know the truth of God's law so as freely to choose and accept it. Conscience, sin, and human morality, which are closely linked to the issues of truth, freedom, and God's law, are among the other important themes with which John Paul II deals.

The Pope exposes the abuses of some theologians who interpret human freedom, conscience, and moral deeds in a manner contrary to the teaching of the Church. This is why he aims his encyclical at the bishops of the Catholic Church who are responsible for the purity of faith in their dioceses.

While criticizing the preferences of the contemporary world, John Paul II stresses the need for human openness to eternal truth. He believes that this lack of openness constitutes a threat to anyone, and this may lead to ideological disorientation, moral enslavement, and consequently, even loss of eternal life. He points to a common tendency of subjectively evaluating the morality of human behavior. This happens when some abstract, universal humanism or socio-political ideology replaces God's law as the basis for morality. The Pope states the fact that no human being has the right to define what is good and what is evil. He reminds us that God has reserved this privilege to himself. After creating the first man, God said to him: "You are free to eat from any of the trees of the garden except the tree of knowledge of good and bad. From that tree you shall not eat; the moment you eat from it you are surely doomed to die" (Gen 2:16–17). This divine prohibition is still valid today, and therefore the Pope reminds us that "the behavioural sciences, despite the great value of the information which they provide, cannot be considered decisive indications of moral norms" (*VS* 112).

While reflecting on the issues related to human morality, John Paul II reminds us that God expects deeds accomplished in accordance with his law. The Holy Father backs his claim with the words of Saint Paul: "Do not be deceived; neither fornicators nor idolaters nor adulterers nor boy prostitutes nor sodomites nor thieves nor the greedy nor drunkards nor slanderers nor robbers will inherit the kingdom of God" (1 Cor 6:9–10).

The main objective of the current encyclical is to inculcate people with a healthy knowledge of morality, providing them with spiritual powers for use in winning the greatest battle of the contemporary world taking place in human consciences: the battle between ideological lawlessness on one side, and God and his law on the other.

"Teacher, What Good Must I Do to Gain Eternal Life?"
(Mt 19:16)

Jesus' conversation with a rich young man is one of the most telling biblical scenes to which John Paul II refers near the beginning of *Veritatis Splendor*. The rich young man of the Gospel story could not find peace of heart despite his considerable material wealth. He was looking for an answer to the question about the good he needed to do to gain eternal life. Jesus reminded him about keeping God's commandments. The young man eagerly wanted to know which ones in particular. Jesus replied: " 'You shall not murder; You shall not commit adultery; You shall not steal; You shall not bear false witness; Honour your father and your mother'; and 'You shall love your neighbor as yourself' " (Mt 16:18–19, in *VS* 6).

Even though there are more of God's commandments, Jesus mentioned only the ones listed above so as to show the young man the way to salvation. The Pope remarks that in spite of the fact that the young man confirmed his observance of God's commandments, he avoided any question related to concrete moral principles. Oftentimes it is frequently more convenient not to ask about it. People can be convinced about their own perfection because of their external observance of the commandments, yet live immorally at the same time. While keeping God's commandments, we must also believe in the God who provided them and listen to him so as to understand how to interpret these commandments, then live in a "proactive" or positive way, not based on the negative "Thou shalt nots," which can easily be rationalized into "as long as I strictly observe the 'Thou shalt nots,' I can do anything else I want." We should listen to God in the community of the Church because where two or three are gathered in Jesus' name, Jesus promised to be among them (see Mt 18:20).

The young man of the gospel asked about the final result for observance of God's commandments—about the attainment of eternal life. Jesus explained to the young man that God's commandments help people attain spiritual and moral liberation both from the falsification of their consciences and from various forms of moral enslavement. God liberates individuals and entire societies. He states this truth at the beginning of the Decalogue: "I, the LORD, am your God, who brought you out of the land of Egypt, that place of slavery. You shall not have other gods besides me" (Ex 20:2–3).

A more important truth is hidden in Jesus' answer to the young man. When the youth asked about the good he was to do, Jesus immediately suggested that only God was good. If this is the case, then human deeds should reflect God's goodness. They should be full of love and justice, and be carried out in kindness and selflessness. Consequently, our morally good deeds are conditioned both by the observance of God's commandments and by close communion with Christ. John Paul II emphasizes in his encyclical what he said at the beginning of his pontificate, that is, that "the man who wishes to understand himself thoroughly . . . must with his unrest, uncertainty and even his weakness and sinfulness, with his life and death, draw near to Christ . . . in order to find himself" (*VS* 8).

The commandments of God's Decalogue refer both to God and to people. The Pope reminds us that the aim of the seven commandments that relate to one's neighbor is "to safeguard the good of the person, the image of God, by protecting his goods. 'You shall not murder; You shall not commit adultery; You shall not steal; You shall not bear false witness'" (*VS* 13). Coming close to Jesus and receiving his grace, which enables us to observe God's commandments, should be a challenge to each one of us. This is the reason why it is so important for us to receive Jesus' invitation that the young man heard: "Come, follow me" (Mt 19:21, in *VS* 11).

God's Law Defines Human Morality

John Paul II in his encyclical writes openly that a contemporary crisis among the faithful consists in negating or undermining the interzonal activity between faith and morality by denying one or the other. The author is aware that conditions of human life have changed, but he unequivocally stresses that divine law is immutable. No representative of the Church who proclaims the gospel or teaches Catholic doctrine on faith and morals can change anything at will. If he were to do it, he would be the smallest in the kingdom of God, according to Jesus' warning (see Mt 18:6).

In many places in his encyclical, the Pope underlines the fundamental truth that God is the creator of moral law. This truth is well illustrated in the following words of the Vatican Council II Constitution *Gaudium et Spes*: "In the depths of his conscience man detects a law which he does not impose on himself, but which holds him to obedience. Always summoning him to love good and avoid evil, the voice of conscience can when necessary speak to his heart more specifically: 'do this, shun that'. For man has in his heart a law written by God. To obey it is the very dignity of man; according to it he will be judged (see: Rom 2:14–16)" (*Gaudium et Spes* 16 in *VS* 54).

John Paul II notices the unfortunate fact that, in spite of the Church's warnings, some false theological tendencies "have led to a denial, in opposition to Sacred Scripture (see Mt 15:3–6) and the Church's constant teaching, of the fact that the natural moral law has God as its author, and that man, by the use of reason, participates in the eternal law, which it is not for him to establish" (*VS* 36).

Being aware of the divine origin of moral law, the Pope demands that this truth should also find its place in the evangelizing proclamation of the

Church. In his view, a clear model of morality is needed to oppose liberal trends that aim at blurring it. He does not make compromises with the spirit of the world and calls on us to stand by God and his law. The Holy Father backs up his call with the words of Saint Paul: "Do not conform yourselves to this age" (Rom 12:2), using these words as the title of the second chapter of his encyclical.

Building earthly reality without reference to God's law constitutes a threat that humanity might end up uprooted from reality and be annihilated. Therefore John Paul II warns, using the words of *Gaudium et Spes*: "Without its Creator the creature simply disappears" (*VS* 39). John Paul II calls everyone, the teaching office of the Church in particular, to vigilance in proclaiming Christian morality. The Pope quotes the words of Saint Paul the Apostle in order to appeal to us: "Preach the word, be urgent in season and out of season; convince, rebuke and exhort, be unfailing in patience and in teaching. For the time will come when people will not endure sound doctrine but, having itching ears they will accumulate for themselves teachers to suit their own likings, and will turn away from the truth and will wander into myths" (2 Tim 4:2–5, in *VS* 30).

John Paul II is convinced that God guides the whole world and the lives of all people. This is the reason why, while talking about God's law, he directs us to our conscience, which should lead each of us to deeds that are morally upright and provide full self-knowledge.

Conscience and Truth

One of the fundamental truths that John Paul II deals with in his encyclical is the issue of conscience. What is conscience? The Pope, who often refers to the teachings of the Second Vatican Council in his documents, gives a definition of conscience based on this particular source. Conscience is the most secret center and "the sanctuary of man, where he is alone with God whose voice echoes within him" (*Gaudium et Spes* 16, in *VS* 55). This definition unequivocally states the truth that in our conscience we must listen to God, and not decide for ourselves what is morally good or evil.

Obviously, the Pope understands the complexity of moral problems in contemporary society. He is aware that conscience expresses the whole of our personality and is linked to our human nature. To make his teaching clearer, however, he quotes a definition of conscience given by Saint Bonaventure as well: "Conscience is like God's herald and messenger; it does not command things on its own authority, but commands them as coming from God's authority, like a herald when he proclaims the edict of the king. This is why conscience has binding force" (*II Librum Sentent.*, dist. 39, a. 1, q. 3, conclusion, in *VS* 58).

It is very clear to John Paul II that contemporary ethical relativism leads to absolute liberty of moral choices. He states, namely, that human conscience must be properly formed on the basis of objective moral norms flowing from God's law. The author expresses this idea in the following words: "The judgment of conscience is a practical judgment, a judgment which makes known what man must do or not do, or which assesses an act already performed by him. It is a judgment which applies to a concrete situation the rational conviction that one must love and do good and avoid evil. . . . But whereas the natural law discloses the objective and universal demands of the moral good, conscience is the application of the law to a particular case" (*VS* 59).

John Paul II points to the fact that the human conscience is constantly threatened with the danger of error. He reminds us of what the Constitution *Gaudium et Spes* said: "Not infrequently conscience can be mistaken as a result of invincible ignorance" (*GS* 16, in *VS* 62). Therefore the Pope teaches that it is the duty of every adult to seek the truth concerning moral norms. Those who break communion with the Church and behave according to their distorted consciences are not dispensed from moral responsibility for their deeds. Subjective evaluation of life and behavior frequently leads people to the mistaken conviction about their grandeur and sinlessness. John Paul points to divine revelation to teach us these truths: "Certainly, in order to have a 'good conscience' (1 Tim 1:5), man must seek the truth and must make judgments in accordance with that same truth. As the Apostle Paul says, the conscience must be 'confirmed by the Holy Spirit' (cf. Rom 9:1); it must be 'clear' (2 Tim 1:3); it must not 'practise cunning and tamper with God's word', but 'openly state the truth' (cf. 2 Cor 4:2)" (*VS* 62).

The Pope also points to the fact that that those who do evil unknowingly, that is, when their conscience is not properly formed, do not bear the same responsibility had they done something against the voice of their consciences. Yet even in this case, evil remains evil, and it makes the moral growth of those who commit those evil deeds impossible (see *VS* 63). The Holy Father strongly emphasizes that conscience is capable of correctly discovering the border between good and evil only if it is rooted in truth. The author encourages us to reflect on Jesus' words: "He who does what is true comes to the light" (Jn 3:21, in *VS* 64).

Freedom and Law

The Pope openly admits the greatest drama in the moral life of contemporary men and women features freedom and law as main actors. He sees the reason for this state of affairs as an incorrect understanding of both law and freedom. He observes that freedom is true only when the person exercising it makes reference to good and truth. This is the reason why he firmly opposes the tendencies of some theologians to separate human freedom from God's law. He does not want to accept the views of those who exalt freedom "almost to the point of idolatry . . . [because it leads] to a *'creative' understanding of moral conscience*, which diverges from the teaching of the Church's tradition and her Magisterium" (*VS* 54). Creativity of conscience means freedom to interpret God's law by any human being who, by virtue of being free, claims the right to do it.

John Paul II turns our attention to the erroneous moral theory called the "fundamental option" (*VS* 65). Some theologians claim that it is enough to make a basic or fundamental choice in favor of God and his law, and then behave according to one's own opinion in particular cases, such as sexuality, without feeling guilty of committing sin. Such an understanding of freedom leads to moral relativism and spiritual disorientation. Therefore, the Pope presents the teaching of the Church, referring to section 17 of the Post-Synodal Apostolic Exhortation *Reconciliatio et Paenitentia* of 1984: "With every freely committed mortal sin, he [man] offends God as the giver of the law and as a result becomes guilty with regard to the entire law (cf. Jas 2:8–11); even if he perseveres in faith, he loses 'sanctifying grace', 'charity' and 'eternal happiness' " (*VS* 68).

The Holy Father notes that the human desire to do good and search for truth finds its expression in freedom. He strongly asserts the fact that the acceptance of God's law does not limit a human being in any way. He expresses this idea in the following words: "Man's *genuine moral autonomy* in no way means the rejection but rather the acceptance of the moral law, of God's command: 'The Lord God gave this command to the man . . .' (Gen 2:16). *Human freedom and God's law meet and are called to intersect,* in the sense of man's free obedience to God and of God's completely gratuitous benevolence towards man" (*VS* 41).

The human vocation to freedom is found in the major themes of God's revelation: "You were called for freedom, brethren" (Gal 5:13), proclaims the Apostle Paul with joy and pride. But he immediately adds, "only do not use this freedom as an opportunity for the flesh" (Gal 5:13, in *VS* 17). The rejection of this truth leads to the falsification of freedom. Therefore the Pope always makes reference to revealed truth when he speaks about human freedom. In this way, he wants to prevent the erroneous use of freedom that ultimately results in its loss. He warns us against it at the very beginning of his encyclical:

> As a result of that mysterious original sin, committed at the prompting of Satan, the one who is "a liar and the father of lies" (Jn 8:44), man is constantly tempted to turn his gaze away from the living and true God in order to direct it towards idols (cf. 1 Thes 1:9), exchanging "the truth about God for a lie" (Rom 1:25). Man's capacity to know the truth is also darkened, and his will to submit to it is weakened. Thus, giving himself over to relativism and scepticism (cf. Jn 18:38), he goes off in search of an illusory freedom apart from truth itself. (*VS* 1)

Mortal and Venial Sin

The Holy Father, being the Vicar of Christ, unequivocally presents the teaching of the Church concerning mortal and venial sin. He firmly rejects the theories of some theologians who claim that the person who chose God by making the so-called fundamental option cannot commit a grave sin. The Pope teaches that the basic human choice in favor of God is a positive act of faith because in this choice "man makes a total and free self-commitment to God, offering 'the full submission of intellect and will to God as he reveals'" (*VS* 66, referring to the Vatican Council II Constitution *Dei Verbum* 5). John Paul II, however, does not accept the views of some theologians who separate the fundamental option for God from conscious choices of particular deeds. He states that similar views contradict, if not reject, the Catholic teaching on mortal sin. A minor or venial sin appears in human life only incidentally, according to those theologians. The Pope, instead, teaches that every consciously performed act comes under moral scrutiny.

John Paul II recalls the Synod of Bishops of 1983 in his reflection. The fruit of this synod was the Apostolic Exhortation *Reconciliatio et Paenitentia* of 1984, which confirmed the teaching of the Synod of Trent (1545–1563) about the clear distinctions between mortal and venial sins. The Pope quotes this document expressing the teaching of the Church on mortal sin: "With the whole tradition of the Church, we call mortal sin the act by which man freely and consciously rejects God, his law, the covenant of love that God offers, preferring to turn in on himself or to some created and finite reality, something contrary to the divine will (*conversio ad creaturam*). This can occur in a direct and formal way, in the sins of idolatry, apostasy and atheism; or in an equivalent way, as in every act of disobedience to God's commandments in a grave matter" (*RP* 17, in *VS* 70).

John Paul II identifies the reason for falsifying basic ideas about a human being and morality: it lies in the separation of freedom from truth. Christ's words about it are recorded in the Gospel of Saint John: "You will know the truth, and the truth will set you free" (Jn 8:32). These words are valid for each one of us today. Those who exercise their freedom without the truth about themselves risk self-destruction. John Paul II in his encyclical firmly states:

> it is never lawful, even for the gravest reasons, to do evil that good may come of it (see Rom 3:8). . . . The Second Vatican Council itself, in discussing the respect due to the human person, gives a number of examples of such acts: "Whatever is hostile to life itself, such as any kind of homicide, genocide, abortion, euthanasia and voluntary suicide; whatever violates the integrity of the human person, such as mutilation, physical and mental torture and attempts to coerce the spirit; whatever is offensive to human dignity, such as subhuman living conditions, arbitrary imprisonment, deportation, slavery, prostitution and trafficking in women and children; degrading conditions of work which treat laborers as mere instruments of profit, and not as free responsible persons: all these and the like are a disgrace, and so long as they infect human civilization they contaminate those who inflict them more than those who suffer injustice, and they are a negation of the honor due to the Creator." (*Gaudium et Spes* 27, in *VS* 80)

The above quotation explains the whole truth about the fact that deeds that are intrinsically evil cannot be justified or "removed" by any "good" intention or any "important" circumstance. Only God can forgive evil deeds, and then only when those who have committed them express their regret and sorrow.

Martyrdom as an Expression of Fidelity to God and His Law

Truth in human life is one of the main themes of the papal encyclical. It gives sense and meaning to human life. The Pope emphasizes that according to Jesus' promise, truth gives us freedom and allows us to remain free in the face of God's authority. It also confers on us the power to accept martyrdom (see *VS* 87). Jesus confirms this in front of Pilate: "For this I was born and for this I came into the world, to testify to the truth" (Jn 18:37). Additionally, Jesus testifies to the truth with his life and, in the name of love, liberates humanity from slavery to sin by means of his death on the Cross (see Phil 2:6–11). Here is the testimony of his saving act: "No one has greater love than this, to lay down one's life for one's friends" (Jn 15:13). The Pope underlines that Christ's testimony is a model and source of power for the disciples who are called to follow in his footsteps: "If anyone wishes to come after me, he must deny himself and take up his cross daily and follow me" (Lk 9:23).

In the history of salvation, we find examples of martyrs who preferred to lose their lives rather than betray God and break his law. We find descriptions of their lives in the books of the Old Testament. A mother and her seven sons took a heroic stance, rejecting the demand of the king's emissaries to commit acts contrary to their consciences and contrary to God's law. They consciously chose to die as martyrs rather than to violate God's law (see 2 Macc 7:1–42). A similar situation happened to Susanna. Two unjust judges craved for her, but she refused to yield to their impure demands. Two elders threatened her with death, but this is what they heard in response: "I am completely trapped. . . . Yet it is better for me to fall into your power without guilt than to sin before the Lord" (Dan 13:22–23). We can clearly see that the Old Testament heroines and heroes were ready to accept martyrdom rather than to do the evil that others wanted to impose on them. Their courage and determination on the way to truth are worthy of greatest admiration and praise.

There were many martyrs in the history of Christianity as well. The first to die a martyr's death was Saint Stephen, who, following Christ's example, prayed for his oppressors (see Acts 8:59–60). A similar fate met John the Baptist because he refused to compromise with evil. The same happened to most of the apostles. The Passion and death of Jesus were for them, just as for other martyrs, the source of strength at the time of suffering and death. Should we not do the same, especially at the hour of trial, instead of talking about the senselessness of suffering?

Martyrs give us the example of love and fidelity offered to Christ. They are authentic models for imitating Jesus' deeds and being inspired by his courage. John Paul II expresses this idea as follows: "The martyrs and, in general, all the Church's Saints, light up every period of history by reawakening its moral sense. By witnessing fully to the good, they are a living reproof to those who transgress the law (cf. Wis 2:12), and they make the words of the Prophet echo ever afresh: 'Woe to those who call evil good and good evil, who put darkness for light and light for darkness, who put bitter for sweet and sweet for bitter!' (Is 5:20)" (*VS* 93). At this point of his encyclical, the Holy Father John Paul II calls us to unite faith with true morality in our daily lives.

Morality and the Renewal of Social Life

The true crisis described by John Paul II in the Encyclical *Veritatis Splendor* touches primarily moral doctrine itself, which in turn influences all spheres of social life. With great concern, the Pope draws our attention to "the *lack of harmony between the traditional response of the Church and certain theological positions*, encountered even in Seminaries and in Faculties of Theology, *with regard to questions of the greatest importance* for the Church and for the life of faith of Christians, as well as for the life of society itself" (*VS* 4).

The Pope believes that, regardless of cultural or social differences, Christians should speak one language of faith, love, and morals, which are imposed on them by the gospel. To illustrate his idea, the Pope recalls the first Christians, who were of both Jewish and pagan cultures and differed from nonbelievers not only in their faith and liturgy but also in their behavior, which was governed by moral principles.

The author of the encyclical tells us: "No damage must be done to the *harmony between faith and life*" (*VS* 26) under any pretext. He is aware of the fact, however, that a secular liberal trend of contemporary culture eliminates moral values and proclaims they do not apply in public life. Faced with this doctrine, the Church cannot make a compromise. John Paul II argues that "the Church's firmness in defending the universal and unchanging moral norms is not demeaning at all. Its only purpose is to serve man's true freedom" (*VS* 96). The Holy Father constantly maintains that the commandments of the Decalogue regulate social life, and "*are the first necessary step on the journey towards freedom*" (*VS* 13). These commandments require that people live their lives without such sins as murder, adultery, debauchery, theft, lies, or blasphemy. When one avoids these sins, "one begins to lift up one's head towards freedom. But this is only the beginning of freedom, not perfect freedom . . . ," as Saint Augustine said (*VS* 13). Additionally, the Pope teaches us with the declaration *Dignitatis Humanae*, from the Second Vatican Council: "there exists a prior moral obligation, and a grave one at that, to seek the truth and to adhere to it once it is known" (*VS* 34).

The Pope also remarks that in contemporary culture "there is a tendency to grant to the individual conscience the prerogative of independently determining the criteria of good and evil and then acting accordingly. Such an outlook is quite congenial to an individualist ethic, wherein each individual is faced with his own truth, different from the truth of others. Taken to its extreme consequences, this individualism leads to a denial of the very idea of human nature" (*VS* 32). If then God's revelation about the human being, natural law, conscience, truth, and human freedom undergoes so much deformation, no wonder that contemporary culture—called the "culture of death" by the Pope—tends to destroy the beauty of the created world and will lead to the annihilation of humanity. The only hope lies in God, who constantly renews humanity and teaches us love.

This is the reason why the Holy Father frequently states that only God, who is the greatest Good, constitutes the solid foundation and irreplaceable source of morality: "Only upon this truth is it possible to construct a renewed society and to solve the complex and weighty problems affecting it" (*VS* 99). He also emphasizes that in all spheres of life—individual, family, social, and political—morality based on truth can render a great service "for society and its genuine development" (*VS* 101).

11 The Gospel of Life (*Evangelium Vitae*)

March 25, 1995

Introduction

T HE VALUE and inviolability of human life are the main themes of John Paul II's eleventh encyclical, *Evangelium Vitae* (*The Gospel of Life*). He laments the tragedy of contemporary culture, which denigrates human life by its approval of unborn baby slaughter and the practice of euthanasia. He justifiably calls this the "culture of death." Opposing this type of "culture," the Pope in his document promulgates holiness of life from its very beginning at conception until its very end at the moment of natural death. These are his words: "Human life is sacred because from its beginning it involves 'the creative action of God, and it remains forever in a special relationship with the Creator, who is its sole end. God alone is the Lord of life from its beginning until its end: no one can, in any circumstance, claim for himself the right to destroy directly an innocent human being'" (Congregation for the Doctrine of Faith, *Donum Vitae* 5, in *EV* 53).

After a thorough analysis of all aspects for the sanctity and dignity of human life, the Holy Father reveals the origins of this tragic and threatening phenomenon that he consistently brands the "culture of death" (*EV* 12). The author sees the root cause of this evil in the false and individualistic understanding of human freedom and in the disregard of God. He writes, namely, that the consequences of pushing God out of society are extremely grave because "when the sense of God is lost, there is also a tendency to lose the sense of man, of his dignity and his life" (*EV* 21). In these cases when the sense of God is lost, people allow their consciences to be distorted by the influences of contemporary, often godless, culture and thus more easily break God's laws, including the very important fifth commandment: "Do not kill!"

The fact that the most important human right, the right to life, becomes an object of negotiation can be considered an extreme example of the aberrations of contemporary culture, according to the Pope. He speaks about it in the following way:

> Democracy, contradicting its own principles, effectively moves towards a form of totalitarianism. The State is no longer the "common home" where all can live together on the basis of principles of fundamental equality, but is transformed into a tyrant State, which arrogates to itself the right to dispose of the life of the weakest and most defenseless members, from the unborn child to the elderly, in the name of a public interest which is really nothing but the interest of one part.
>
> The appearance of the strictest respect for legality is maintained, at least when the laws permitting abortion and euthanasia are the result of a ballot in accordance with what are generally seen as the rules of democracy. Really, what we have here is only the tragic caricature of legality; the democratic ideal, which is only truly such when it acknowledges and safeguards the dignity of every human person, is betrayed in its very foundations. (*EV* 20).

When John Paul II talks about a specific "conspiracy against life" (*EV* 12), he wishes to sensitize the consciences of lawmakers and to awaken their sense of responsibility. Special attention should be paid here to the biblical warning that is very closely related: "We must obey God rather than men" (Acts 5:29, in *EV* 67).

The Inviolability of Human Life—"Do Not Kill!"

All major religious traditions and even the most purely secular worldviews value human life in a special way. Doctors testify to this fact when they comply with the Hippocratic oath, to give but one example. Pope John Paul II honestly confesses that one of the motivations for writing *Evangelium Vitae* was the request of bishops and cardinals who demanded the Pope, through the authority of his office, confirm the worth and sacredness of human life. The author speaks about it in the following words:

"The present Encyclical, the fruit of the cooperation of the Episcopate of every country of the world, is therefore meant to be a precise and vigorous reaffirmation of the value of human life and its inviolability, and at the same time a pressing appeal addressed to each and every person, in the name of God: respect, protect, love and serve life, every human life! Only in this direction will you find justice, development, true freedom, peace and happiness!" (*EV* 5).

The Pope reminds us that every person who is honestly open to goodness and truth can recognize the holiness of life inscribed in his heart (see Gen 2:14–15), from conception until natural death according to natural law, thanks to the enlightenment of the mind and under the mysterious influence of grace. This is the reason why John Paul II addresses the present encyclical on the "gospel of life" not only to the faithful but all people of the world (*EV* 101). He is, namely, convinced about "the right of every human being to have this primary good respected to the highest degree" (*EV* 2).

Touching on the issues related to the inviolability of human life, John Paul II clearly points to the individual responsibility before God of those who kill others, including unborn babies. God's words to Noah after the flood provide an excellent illustration here: "I will demand an accounting . . . and from man in regard to his fellow man I will demand an accounting for human life" (Gen 9:5). The truth about the value of human life is included in God's plan because God called people to eternity: "For God formed man to be imperishable; in the image of his own nature he made him" (Wis 2:23). In the following verse, the same biblical author indicates the key reasons for murder of anyone by another, namely, is prior sin, and the originator of sin, namely Satan: "But by the envy of the devil, death entered the world, and they who are in his possession experience it" (Wis 2:24).

We all know the biblical story of Abel who was killed by his brother Cain (Gen 4:1–16). The Pope describes the process of sin taking its roots in the human heart while analyzing the attitude of Cain. Before the murder, Cain walked with a gloomy face. God asked him: "Why are you so resentful and crestfallen? If you do well, you can hold up your head; but if not, sin is a demon lurking at the door: his urge is toward you, yet you can be his master" (Gen 4:6–7).

After the murder, God knew well what had taken place, but he asked Cain, "Where is your brother Abel?" (Gen 4:9). By asking this question,

God gave Cain a chance to express remorse and sorrow for the sin and to begin the process of conversion. John Paul II, while analyzing this scene, refers to the *Catechism of the Catholic Church* where it is written: "In the account of Abel's murder by his brother Cain, Scripture reveals the presence of anger and envy in man, consequences of original sin, from the beginning of human history. Man has become the enemy of his fellow man" (*CCC* 2259, in *EV* 8). God gives life to people and protects this life with the fifth commandment: "Do not kill!"

Abortion and Euthanasia Deny the Right to Life

Independent of the fact that the contemporary world distorts the concept of freedom, one must be aware that in any case of a performed abortion or euthanasia, we will face the consequences of such an act directly before God, and we will have to answer for the killing of a human being. Criminal law does not always agree with moral law. Observance of criminal law does not dispense us from the responsibility for our deeds before God. Our behavior should comply with God's law, that is, with our conscience. Whenever human law conflicts with God's law, it ceases to be binding in conscience. The Pope explains this issue: "Abortion and euthanasia are thus crimes which no human law can claim to legitimize. There is no obligation in conscience to obey such laws; instead there is a grave and clear obligation to oppose them by conscientious objection" (*EV* 73).

John Paul II also notes that some democratic societies justify abortion citing difficult circumstances in the lives of future parents. The Pope, as the Vicar of Christ, is not afraid of calling things by their name, and in his document speaks about it in a unequivocal manner:

> We shall concentrate particular attention on another category of attacks, affecting life in its earliest and in its final stages, attacks which present new characteristics with respect to the past. . . . It is not only that in generalized opinion these attacks tend no longer to be considered as "crimes"; paradoxically they assume the nature of "rights", to the point that the State is called upon to give them legal recognition and to make them available through the free services of health-care personnel. Such attacks strike human life at the time of its greatest frailty, when it lacks any means of self-defence. (*EV* 11)

One of the fundamental human rights is the right to life. It is therefore incomprehensible why some contemporary democratic societies violate this right. The Pope expresses this idea in the following way: "The process which once led to discovering the idea of 'human rights'—rights inherent in every person and prior to any Constitution and State legislation—is today marked by a surprising contradiction. Precisely in an age when the inviolable rights of the person are solemnly proclaimed and the value of life is publicly affirmed, the very right to life is being denied or trampled upon, especially at the more significant moments of existence: the moment of birth and the moment of death" (*EV* 18).

The facts described by the Pope indicate a totally new concept of law, which is adjusted to the opinions of individuals. The Pope says: "In the democratic culture of our time it is commonly held that the legal system of any society should limit itself to taking account of and accepting the convictions of the majority. It should therefore be based solely upon what the majority itself considers moral and actually practises" (*EV* 69). He highlights another worrying phenomenon: the loss of the ability to think in ethical categories, which affects an increasing number of people, with consequent malformation of their consciences. In this way, they destroy the reference to the moral law that is inscribed in the heart of every person and oppose concrete moral values contained in the Decalogue. Acceptance of a degenerated form of freedom, making lawlessness a moral norm, and disregard of the divine law are very dangerous phenomena that threaten not only the lives of other people, but also social development and true democracy as well.

Civil Law and Moral Law

The author refers to his predecessors on a number of occasions to ensure the continuity of the teaching of the Church on moral issues. Writing about the relationship between civil and moral laws, John Paul II quotes John XXIII's Encyclical *Pacem in Terris* and Saint Thomas Aquinas's *Summa theologiae*. In the first document, we find the following teaching: "Authority is a postulate of the moral order and derives from God. Consequently, laws and decrees enacted in contravention of the moral order, and hence of the divine will, can have no binding force in conscience. . . . Indeed, the passing of such laws undermines the very nature of authority and results in shameful abuse" (*Pacem in Terris*, 51). Saint Thomas teaches in a similar way: " 'Human law is law inasmuch as it is in conformity with right reason and thus derives from the eternal law. But when a law is contrary to reason, it is called an unjust law; but in this case it ceases to be a law and becomes instead an act of violence.' And again: 'Every law made by man can be called a law insofar as it derives from the natural law. But if it is somehow opposed to the natural law, then it is not really a law but rather a corruption of the law' " (*Summa theologiae*, in *EV* 72).

John Paul II underlines that the above teaching refers in the first place to human legislation that does not recognize the basic and primordial right of every human being to life. Consequently, laws that permit direct killing of innocent human beings through abortion or euthanasia remain in total and permanent contradiction with the inviolable right to life proper to every person. In this way, these laws deny the equality of all people before the law (see *EV* 72).

The Pope stresses that no person can have power over human life, or the authority to decide and define the moment an embryo becomes a human being. Contemporary molecular biology and genetics have provided sufficient and important information proving that at the moment of fertilization of an ovum with a sperm a new genetic structure is formed—a new human being is created.

The emergence of the so-called double standard morality testifies to deep moral relativism. The issues related to life, abortion, euthanasia, or contraception are treated as private matters, and personal opinion deformed by the influence of the "culture of death" has the final say on what is acceptable. According to the teaching of God safeguarded by the Church, on the other hand, all people are obliged to follow the law inscribed in their consciences that is fulfilled through the love for God and neighbor.

In relation to the above, the Holy Father pays particular attention to the conflicts of conscience taking place in the hearts of honest lawmakers. It is obvious that a member of a legislature who follows the voice of conscience should never support a law that allows abortion or euthanasia. The Pope remarks: "In the case of an intrinsically unjust law . . . it is . . . never licit to obey it, or to 'take part in a propaganda campaign in favour of such a law, or vote for it' " (Congregation for the Doctrine of the Faith, Declaration on Procured Abortion, no. 22 in *EV* 73). In case a lawmaker is not in the position to abrogate a law on abortion, he or she "could licitly support proposals aimed at limiting the harm done by such a law" (*EV* 73).

To sum up the present chapter, it is necessary to underline and remember that under no circumstances should civil law be allowed to take the place of conscience.

Natural Family Planning as Opposed to Contraception

Apart from holiness and inviolability of human life, John Paul II in *Evangelium Vitae* touches on the issues related to moral principles applicable in the transmission of life. He calls a family that uses natural methods of spacing births a "sanctuary of life" (*EV* 6) because it is ready to welcome every new human life that God grants. God created a man and a woman so that thanks to their love life might continue on earth. The Pope mentions the emergence of numerous organizations, both in the Church and in society as a whole, that support and help in planning the spacing of children or parenting decisions. He writes: "Centres for natural methods of regulating fertility should be promoted as a valuable help to responsible parenthood. . . . Marriage and family counselling agencies by their specific work of guidance and prevention . . . also offer valuable help in rediscovering the meaning of love and life" (*EV* 88). Human life is God's gift, but God chose to make this gift dependent on human cooperation: "If it is true that human life is in the hands of God, it is no less true that these are loving hands, like those of a mother who accepts, nurtures and takes care of her child" (*EV* 39).

John Paul II draws our attention to the fact that although the service of life is a vast and complex domain, every family is called to take particular care of life, and to deepen the sense of parenthood. The Holy Father appeals to families to take great care of children from other families who are unwanted or neglected. He expresses this in beautiful words: "A particularly significant expression of solidarity between families is a willingness to adopt or take in children abandoned by their parents or in situations of serious hardship" (*EV* 93).

The Pope also points to the natural method of family planning as opposed to contraception, the latter being immoral. He observes that there exists a tendency to deny the link between contraception and abortion. He conveys this idea as follows: "It is frequently asserted that contraception, if made safe and available to all, is the most effective remedy against abortion. The Catholic Church is then accused of actually promoting abortion, because she obstinately continues to teach the moral unlawfulness of contraception. . . . Indeed, the pro-abortion culture is especially strong precisely where the Church's teaching on contraception is rejected" (*EV* 13).

Natural family planning should, according to John Paul II's advice, help married partners discover the essence of their love as a gift in both physical and spiritual dimensions and bring them closer to the creative presence of God in the new life being born in their family. The Holy Father phrases this lofty thought in the following words:

> As I wrote in my "Letter to Families": When a new person is born of the conjugal union of the two, he brings with him into the world a particular image and likeness of God himself: the genealogy of the person is inscribed in the very biology of generation. In affirming that the spouses, as parents, cooperate with God the Creator in conceiving and giving birth to a new human being, we are not speaking merely with reference to the laws of biology. Instead, we wish to emphasize that God himself is present in human fatherhood and motherhood. (*EV* 43)

The Pope states that the encouragement to use natural family planning methods expressed in the encyclical is addressed not to the faithful alone but also to all people living on our planet (see *EV* 101).

Euthanasia as Lack of Love for Human Life

This encyclical of John Paul II, *Evangelium Vitae—The Gospel of Life—* can also be called "The Gospel of Love" because it refers to Jesus. The deepest indication of human dignity is the fact that each person is loved by God in Jesus. In Saint John's Gospel, we read: "For God so loved the world that he gave his only Son, so that everyone who believes in him might not perish but might have eternal life" (3:16). The Pope reminds us that "It is precisely by his death that Jesus reveals all the splendor and value of life, inasmuch as his self-oblation on the Cross becomes the source of new life for all people" (cf. Jn 12:32; *EV* 33). It is in God, then, that we find strength to accept and love the life that he gives us, and this love refers to both our own life and to the life of other human beings.

John Paul II explains that an attack on human life, both before a person's birth as well as in old age, has its roots in the weakening of the sense of God, and in the disregard for true values proper to the human person, which in effect "inevitably leads to a practical materialism. . . . The so-called 'quality of life' is interpreted primarily or exclusively as economic efficiency, inordinate consumerism, physical beauty and pleasure, to the neglect of the more profound dimensions—interpersonal, spiritual and religious—of existence" (*EV* 23).

The manner in which the Holy Father accepted his own death many years after writing this encyclical not only showed us the true sense of human suffering but also revealed the deep love for life that he cherished.

The Pope in his document reminds us also that love is the most important commandment of God. This is the reason why human life should be defended until natural death. He conveys this thought in the following words: "The meaning of life is found in giving and receiving love, and in this light human sexuality and procreation reach their true and full significance. Love also gives meaning to suffering and death" (*EV* 81).

Suffering, especially when caused by serious and prolonged illness, is always a problem for the sick and for their families. The Pope teaches, however, that human life is good and precious because it is a gift from God. He affirms: "Even pain and suffering have meaning and value when they are experienced in close connection with love received and given. In this regard, I have called for the yearly celebration of the World Day of the Sick, emphasizing 'the salvific nature of the offering up of suffering which, experienced in communion with Christ, belongs to the very essence of the Redemption'" (*EV* 97, quoting the Letter establishing the World Day of the Sick, May 13, 1992).

Instead of focusing on the negative sides of sickness and old age, John Paul II points to the many positive aspects of advanced age and infirmity. He lists the enrichment of family connections between generations as one of these benefits. He phrases the idea in the following way: "The elderly are not only to be considered the object of our concern, closeness and service. They themselves have a valuable contribution to make to the Gospel of life. Thanks to the rich treasury of experiences they have acquired through the years, the elderly can and must be sources of wisdom and witnesses of hope and love" (*EV* 94). At times, however, the opposite of papal-inspired teaching happens in a family when a sick and frail member is perceived as a useless burden. The temptation to perform euthanasia can arise in such a context.

The Pope repeatedly stresses that a human person is to be treated with love at every stage of his or her life. He reminds us that all our relationships with our neighbors should be considered in constant reference to our faith and the Last Judgment—Jesus said: "As you did it to one of the least of these my brethren, you did it to me" (Mt 25:40, in *EV* 87).

Human Beings Called to the Fullness of Life

John Paul II, aware of the fact that many contemporary people are dragged into a dramatic struggle between the "culture of death" and the "culture of life," invites us to a conscious and firm declaration on the side of life. He clearly points to Jesus who is life (see Jn 14:6), and who desires to bestow the fullness of life on every human being. The author expresses the idea as follows: "The Gospel of life is not simply a reflection . . . on human life. Nor is it merely a commandment aimed at raising awareness and bringing about significant changes in society. Still less is it an illusory promise of a better future. The Gospel of life is something concrete and personal, for it consists in the proclamation of the very person of Jesus" (*EV* 29).

In spite of the existence of many threats to human life in the world today, the Pope firmly believes that the future belongs to the culture of life and love, rather than to the culture of death. He aims at reviving faith by means of his document and making humanity aware that it is called to the "fullness of life," both on earth and in eternity. When introducing the term "fullness of life," he thinks of the following divine gifts: mind, free will, and the ability to love and share with others our material and spiritual goods. We must remember that every person has been showered with spiritual gifts. The correct use of these divine gifts should help people achieve the fullest human development possible here on earth. Another important gift we have received from God is eternal life. The author conveys the essence of this message: "To proclaim Jesus is itself to proclaim life. . . . By the gift of the Spirit, this same life has been bestowed on us. It is in being destined to life in its fullness, to 'eternal life,' that every person's earthly life acquires its full meaning" (*EV* 80).

It is obvious to the Holy Father that sanctity and inviolability of life constitute the foundation of all human gifts and are the basis of our journey toward completeness. He speaks about it very clearly: "Human life is sacred and inviolable at every moment of existence, including the initial phase which precedes birth. All human beings, from their mother's womb, belong to God who searches them and knows them, who forms them and knits them together with his own hands, who gazes on them when they are tiny shapeless embryos and already sees in them the adults of tomorrow whose days are numbered and whose vocation is even now written in the 'book of life' (cf. Ps 139:1, 13–16)" (*EV* 61).

It is only when we are grateful to God for the gift of life, and when we know how to employ and benefit from all our gifts and talents so as to serve others, that we can find contentment and be granted the understanding of the deep sense of our life. When, on the other hand, someone rejects God and claims to have become the sole master of his or her life (treated instrumentally and as a mere object), that person will find neither happiness nor meaning in their existence. John Paul II expresses this very eloquently: "Enclosed in the narrow horizon of his physical nature . . . he no longer considers life as a splendid gift of God. . . . Life itself becomes a mere thing, which man claims as his exclusive property, completely subject to his control and manipulation" (*EV* 22).

People cannot identify themselves with things since they are persons. The Pope reminds us about it with the beautiful words: "All who commit themselves to following Christ are given the fullness of life" (*EV* 36).

A Call to Build a New Culture of Human Life

A new culture of life finds its beginning in Jesus, that is, in the proclamation of the "gospel of life." The faithful who receive Christ as their Lord aspire to have evangelical values permeate all spheres of their lives. It is to a life according to such values that John Paul II invites all people of good will, which is the subject of the last section of his encyclical: "Enlightened by this Gospel of life, we feel a need to proclaim it and to bear witness to it in all its marvelous newness. Since it is one with Jesus himself, who makes all things new and conquers the 'oldness' which comes from sin and leads to death, this Gospel exceeds every human expectation" (*EV* 80).

The Holy Father draws our attention to the fact that the construction of a new culture of life is a very vast and complex endeavor. It is therefore not enough to have only selected individuals involved in the process. He affirms the need and duty of engagement by all: "Everyone has an obligation to be at the service of life. . . . This community commitment does not however eliminate or lessen the responsibility of each individual, called by the Lord to 'become the neighbour' of everyone: 'Go and do likewise' (Lk 10:37)" (*EV* 79).

The author presents and makes familiar only some of the many aspects of human life in his encyclical. Catholic universities are one of these special spheres of his interests, and therefore he writes: "We need to make sure that in theological faculties, seminaries and Catholic institutions sound doctrine is taught, explained and more fully investigated" (*Veritatis Splendor* 116, in *EV* 82).

The Pope also cites the great importance of correctly forming one's conscience. He clearly stresses this idea: "The first and fundamental step towards this cultural transformation consists in forming consciences with regard to the incomparable and inviolable worth of every human life. It is of the greatest importance to re-establish the essential connection between life and freedom. These are inseparable goods: where one is violated, the other also ends up being violated. There is no true freedom where life is not welcomed and loved; and there is no fullness of life except in freedom" (*EV* 96).

The family unit has a fundamental role to play in the construction of a new culture in human life. It is most important when a new human life is born. This is the reason why the Pope calls it "the sanctuary of life" (*EV* 6) and "the domestic church" (*EV* 92); additionally the family is "the place in which life—the gift of God—can be properly welcomed and protected against the many attacks to which it is exposed, and can develop in accordance with what constitutes authentic human growth" (*Centesimus Annus* 39, in *EV* 92). The root of the contemporary crisis of the family is most certainly to be found in the disregard of the gospel of life, and therefore John Paul II appreciates the responsibility of this basic unit of society for life in accordance with the gospel values: "In particular, there is a need for education about the value of life from its very origins. It is an illusion to think that we can build a true culture of human life if we do not help the young to accept and experience sexuality and love and the whole of life according to their true meaning" (*EV* 97).

It is very telling that John Paul II calls not just the faithful but all people to foster and nourish human life. Care for life is a universal concern, and a culture of life can therefore become a focus to unite all humanity. The Pope is optimistic that "we shall find important points of contact and dialogue also with non-believers, in our common commitment to the establishment of a new culture of life" (*EV* 82).

12 That They May Be One (*Ut Unum Sint*)

May 25, 1995

Introduction

CHRISTIAN UNITY was a great desire of John Paul II from the first days of his pontificate. He gave expression to this aspiration first in his expository encyclical *Redemptor Hominis*, then in numerous homilies, as well as ecumenical meetings that he often initiated. The theme of ecumenism is most comprehensively treated in his twelfth encyclical, entitled *Ut Unum Sint* (*That They May Be One*), published on May 25, 1995, the feast of the Ascension of the Lord.

By means of his persistent efforts toward unification of divided Christians, the Holy Father overcame stereotyped prejudices of those among Christ's followers who think that Marian devotion precludes the possibility of any ecumenical commitment. Instead, the Pope amazed the Christian world with his very bold proposals. For example, he did not uphold prior excommunications related to splits in the Church and invites us to treat all Christian communities as "Sister Churches." We find this thought in the following passage: "For centuries we lived this life of 'Sister Churches,' and together held Ecumenical Councils which guarded the deposit of faith against all corruption. And now, after a long period of division and mutual misunderstanding, the Lord is enabling us to discover ourselves as 'Sister Churches' once more, in spite of the obstacles which were once raised between us" (Apostolic Brief *Anno Ineunte* [July 25, 1967], in *UUS* 57).

In the present document, the author draws our attention primarily to those elements of the Christian tradition contributing to unity of the Lord's followers rather than those which divide, as was often the case in prior time, especially in pre–Vatican II Church documents. The Pope stresses that the common factor capable of uniting nearly everyone is universally recognized and honored Baptism. He believes that the Holy Spirit is the first and main creator of unity. John Paul II includes prayer, conversion of the heart, inner transformation, and dialogue as other key factors that can help unite divided Christians. He observes that all Christians are called to a conversion of heart, not just one group or another. He explains:

> The commitment to ecumenism must be based upon the conversion of hearts and upon prayer, which will also lead to the *necessary purification of past memories*. With the grace of the Holy Spirit, the Lord's disciples, inspired by love, by the power of the truth and by a sincere desire for mutual forgiveness and reconciliation, are called to *re-examine together their painful past* and the hurt which that past regrettably continues to provoke even today. All together, they are invited by the ever fresh power of the Gospel to acknowledge with sincere and total objectivity the mistakes made. (*UUS* 2)

John Paul II is aware that the main bone of contention in all ecumenical endeavors is his primacy, that is, his function as successor to the Apostle Peter. This awareness prompts him to become the first and only Pope in history to invite other churches to have a new look at this particular ministry of his. Here is one of the many ways in which he worded this groundbreaking request: "I insistently pray the Holy Spirit to shine his light upon us, enlightening all the Pastors and theologians of our Churches, that we may seek—together, of course—the forms in which this ministry may accomplish a service of love recognized by all concerned" (Homily, Vatican Basilica in the presence of Dimitrios I, Archbishop of Constantinople and Ecumenical Patriarch [December 6, 1987], in *UUS* 95).

Unity in Truth

In his zealous commitment to Christian unity, the Holy Father stresses that all efforts toward this goal have sense only when they are based on truth, and when all followers of Christ seek truth for the common good of humanity. He makes us aware that arbitrary changes in the way we practice our faith made only in order to win over people do not please God in the least. Referring to ecumenical documents of his predecessors, and to those of the Second Vatican Council in particular, he writes:

> Here it is not a question of altering the deposit of faith, changing the meaning of dogmas, eliminating essential words from them, accommodating truth to the preferences of a particular age, or suppressing certain articles of the *Creed* under the false pretext that they are no longer understood today. The unity willed by God can be attained only by the adherence of all to the content of revealed faith in its entirety. In matters of faith, compromise is in contradiction with God who is Truth. In the Body of Christ, "the way, and the truth, and the life" (Jn 14:6), who could consider legitimate a reconciliation brought about at the expense of the truth? (*UUS* 18)

The author desires to be faithful to the truth as revealed by God on one hand, and sensitive to facts in the field of ecumenism accomplished by people on the other. Therefore, he emphasizes in his encyclical a telling fact: "What is essential is the question of faith. The prayer of Christ, our one Lord, Redeemer and Master, speaks to everyone in the same way, both in the East and in the West" (*UUS* 65).

Another dimension of the ecumenical movement to which the Pope points is that many people in various Christian churches undertake concrete efforts toward peace in the world and aim at establishing social justice. These activities have a much broader meaning than just a religious one, in that they foster the unity of the human family. He praises these activities as expressions of a mature faith that is applied in personal, familial, and social spheres of life. We find this idea in the following: "Social and cultural life offers ample opportunities for ecumenical cooperation. With increasing frequency Christians are working together to defend human dignity, to promote peace, to apply the Gospel to social life, to bring the Christian spirit to the world of science and of the arts. They find themselves ever more united in striving to meet the sufferings and the needs of our time: hunger, natural disasters and social injustice" (*UUS* 74).

When it comes to religious life in general, unity in truth is to consist primarily in the recognition of fraternity among all Christians, according to John Paul II. This is to happen despite divisions of the past. Consequently, a mutual request of pardon and forgiveness, as well as the lifting of accusations and age-old prejudices are necessary. Unity in truth does not derive from self-glorification and belittling others, but is based on mutual respect and initiatives aimed at sustaining the atmosphere of God's love. Here are his words: "One of the first steps in ecumenical dialogue is the effort to draw the Christian Communities into this completely interior spiritual space in which Christ, by the power of the Spirit, leads them all, without exception, to examine themselves before the Father" (*UUS* 82).

Fruits of Dialogue for the Sake of Unity

Recent decades of ecumenical dialogue allowed divided Christians to get to know each other better, and to understand more fully the complex historical and religious circumstances that had led to divisions of the Church. The positive element that the Pope prefers is the current trend among young Christians in particular to search for new, practical ways of mutual rapprochement and reconciliation; this is done in view of detailed analyses of the mistakes committed by forefathers. John Paul II speaks about these efforts: "In the eyes of the world, cooperation among Christians becomes a form of common Christian witness and a means of evangelization which benefits all involved" (*UUS* 40).

Additionally, the Pope cites the fact that one of the essential effects of the ecumenical dialogue is the rediscovery of fraternity. He stresses that "in the spirit of the Sermon on the Mount, Christians of one confession no longer consider other Christians as enemies or strangers but see them as brothers and sisters. Again, the very expression *separated brethren* tends to be replaced today by expressions which more readily evoke the deep communion—linked to the baptismal character—which the Spirit fosters in spite of historical and canonical divisions. Today we speak of 'other Christians', 'others who have received Baptism', and 'Christians of other Communities' " (*UUS* 42).

Distinct from recognizing fraternity among Christians of various ecclesial communities, fruitful encounters of key representatives of various churches with the Holy Father are to be considered as yet another success of ecumenical dialogue. John Paul II reminds us that during the Second Vatican Council a breakthrough ecclesial act was approved, namely, a Joint Declaration of Pope Paul VI and the Patriarch of Constantinople

Athenagoras I (Tomos Agapis), "whereby 'there was removed from memory and from the midst of the Church' the remembrance of the excommunications which nine hundred years before, in 1054, had become the symbol of the schism between Rome and Constantinople. That ecclesial event, so filled with ecumenical commitment, took place during the last days of the Council, on 7 December 1965. . . . This gesture had been preceded by the meeting of Pope Paul VI and Patriarch Athenagoras I in Jerusalem, in January 1964, during the Pope's pilgrimage to the Holy Land" (*UUS* 52).

The author of the encyclical, who strives to achieve reconciliation between various church communities by all possible means, seems to be best remembered for his famous saying that "the Church must breathe with her two lungs! In the first millennium of the history of Christianity, this expression refers primarily to the relationship between Byzantium and Rome. From the time of the Baptism of Rus' (Russia) it comes to have an even wider application: evangelization spread to a much vaster area, so that it now includes the entire Church" (*UUS* 54). When the Pope used this comparison, he meant the maintenance of unity between the Eastern and Western Churches. He proclaimed Saints Cyril and Methodius as co-patrons of Europe (together with Saint Benedict) in 1984. This event was closely related to the eleventh centenary of the evangelizing activity of Saints Cyril and Methodius, the Apostles of the Slavs.

The Pope does not stop the ecumenical dialogue with only the East. As a matter of fact, all Christian communities of the world are equally close to his heart. He openly acknowledges that the cordial ecumenical encounters with representatives of other churches accompanied by sincere dialogue made a deep impression on him. With particular fondness, he recalls meeting church leaders in Germany (1980 and 1987), England, Scotland, and Wales (1982), Scandinavian countries (1989), the United States (1984 and 1987), and others. He recalls with emotion the Holy Mass celebrated together with Lutherans in Finland and Sweden: "At Communion time, the Lutheran Bishops approached the celebrant. . . . With love I blessed them" (*UUS* 72).

The Meaning of Primacy in the Context of Church Unity

In the third part of his Encyclical *Ut Unum Sint*, John Paul II speaks about the meaning of his own function as Saint Peter's successor and Bishop of

Rome, and about the role of the papacy in uniting the Church in general. He recalls the act of conferring pastoral primacy on Peter by Jesus as described in John's Gospel (21:15–17), which was harmoniously interpreted by all Christians for the first ten centuries of our faith. In the subsequent centuries, starting from the eleventh, various splits within the Christian communion took place, and each side was guilty of some glaring mistakes. Therefore, the Pope asks for forgiveness on behalf of past shepherds of the Church of Rome. He then sets out to interpret the papal role in a new, truly evangelical manner. He quotes his own noble words, which he first uttered during a solemn meeting with the representatives of other churches at the headquarters of the World Council of Churches in Geneva on June 12, 1984: "To the extent that we are responsible for these I join my Predecessor Paul VI in asking forgiveness" (*UUS* 88).

While discussing the issue of papal primacy, which is theologically based on the privileged status among the Twelve that Jesus gave to Peter, the Holy Father explains its essence: service to God and people; strengthening the followers of Christ in faith; and protecting the integrity of the faith. The service of the pope is related to the attitude assumed by Christ who came to serve and not to be served (see Mt 20:28). Therefore, the descriptive papal title *servus servorum Dei* ("the servant of God's servants") very accurately defines the mission of the pope. A requirement placed on this ministry of the pope is constant conversion and transformation of the heart. John Paul II, who sets this task of repentance and interior change for all Christians, set it firstly for himself. He states the fact that Christ calls everyone to conversion, the pope included. Even though John Paul II has called for general conversion spontaneously and as an expression of his deep faith, it is worthwhile recalling Jesus' words directed to Peter: "I have prayed for you that your faith may not fail; and when you have turned again, strengthen your brethren" (Lk 22:32, in *UUS* 4).

The crucial role played by Saint Peter and his successors as the defenders of Church unity cannot be neglected in any ecumenical considerations. This is why John Paul II reminds us the words of the Vatican Council II Constitution *Lumen Gentium* (23), which speaks of God making Peter a "perpetual and visible principle and foundation of unity" (*UUS* 88). Safeguarding the integrity of faith is the primary mission of Peter and his successors, and they perform it by interpreting the Word of God, explaining the meaning of the holy sacraments, clarifying the mystery of the Church, and highlighting the role of God's Mother in the history of salvation. These issues—and understanding the sacraments of the Eucharist and priesthood in particular—have been interpreted in divergent ways since the time divisions crept in among Christians.

In his desire to accomplish this mission that Christ has entrusted to him, John Paul II affirms:

> In this courageous journey towards unity, the transparency and the prudence of faith require us to avoid both false irenicism [elimination of differences among the churches] and indifference to the Church's ordinances (see *Unitatis Redintegratio* 4 and 11). Conversely, that same transparency and prudence urge us to reject a halfhearted commitment to unity. . . . To uphold a vision of unity which takes account of all the demands of revealed truth does not mean to put a brake on the ecumenical movement. On the contrary, it means preventing it from settling for apparent solutions (see Address to the Cardinals and the Roman Curia [June 28, 1985]). . . . The obligation to respect the truth is absolute. Is this not the law of the Gospel? (*UUS* 79)

Catholic Church and Ecumenism

John Paul II strongly emphasizes that, in accordance with the precepts of the Second Vatican Council, all the faithful of the Catholic Church are called to participate in the ecumenical endeavor. Therefore, he states this effort aimed at Christian unity is not some sort of an addition to the pastoral mission of the Church, but the ecumenical way is the very way of the Church. This same truth about unity as belonging to the essence of the Church is expressed in the document of the Congregation for the Doctrine of the Faith, *Dominus Jesus*.

The following quotation from the conciliar Dogmatic Constitution on the Church has a particularly strong motivational appeal for the Pope when it comes to ecumenical undertakings in the contemporary world, where divisions among Christians are still taking place: "The Council states that the Church of Christ 'subsists in the Catholic Church, which is governed by the Successor of Peter and by the Bishops in communion with him, and at the same time acknowledges that many elements of sanctification and of truth can be found outside her visible structure. These elements, however, as gifts properly belonging to the Church of Christ, possess an inner dynamism towards Catholic unity' " (*Lumen Gentium* 8, in *UUS* 10).

The author of the encyclical firmly believes in the real possibility of unifying all Christians and professing faith in one, holy, catholic, and apostolic Church, founded as she was by Christ himself. The Holy Father believes in the efficacy of ecumenical efforts when they are subject to the powerful action of the Holy Spirit. The following quotation from the conciliar Decree on Ecumenism clearly expresses the Pope's idea: "In all of Christ's disciples the Spirit arouses the desire to be peacefully united, in the manner determined by Christ, as one flock under one shepherd" (*Unitatis Redintegratio* 15, in *UUS* 12).

John Paul II's attitude toward other Christians was strongly characterized by openness. He was always looking for ways of reconciliation among divided followers of Christ in religious, cultural, and social spheres, as well as on the level of personal testimony of individual Christians. This open attitude of the Pope can be seen in the following words:

> Thanks to ecumenism, our contemplation of "the mighty works of God" (*mirabilia Dei*) has been enriched by new horizons . . . : the knowledge that the Spirit is at work in other Christian Communities, the discovery of examples of holiness, the experience of the immense riches present in the communion of saints, and contact with unexpected dimensions of Christian commitment. In a corresponding way, there is an increased sense of the need for repentance: an awareness of certain exclusions which seriously harm fraternal charity, of certain refusals to forgive, of a certain pride, of an unevangelical insistence on condemning the "other side", of a disdain born of an unhealthy presumption. Thus, the entire life of Christians is marked by a concern for ecumenism; and they are called to let themselves be shaped, as it were, by that concern. (*UUS* 15)

The Pope thus outlines both the value and the necessity of ecumenical initiatives of the Church as the only way of fostering authentic spiritual development, and as a means of bringing closer the day of reconciliation, in accordance with Christ's desire expressed in prayer during his hour of Passion: "that they may be one" (Jn 17:21, in *UUS* 9).

Prayer and the Conversion of Heart as Conditions of Unity

John Paul II attaches great value to prayer and the conversion of human hearts in his unceasing attempts toward achieving more profound unity among Christians. The Holy Spirit has wrought modifications to long-established and often negative perceptions about other Christians that may have formed in the minds of the baptized, and these have inspired the Holy Father with great hope for the future. These changes allow people to understand their separated brothers and sisters better, especially when they simply happen to be born to different ecclesial communities. In this regard, he states clearly that the *"fellowship in prayer leads people to look at the Church and Christianity in a new way"* (*UUS* 23). Additionally, he is convinced that prayer and inner conversion of the heart help people do a proper examination of conscience and honestly reflect on their behavior. As the result of such a change, it is easier for them to understand the faults and mistakes of themselves and others, and ultimately forgive these on the basis of this compassionate understanding.

The Pope firmly believes that the Holy Spirit is the creator of unity. This is the reason why he invites everyone to common prayer, which brings closer the goal of unifying Christian communities. John Paul II rejoices greatly over the fact that the prayer for Christian unity has been established not only during ecumenical encounters but also in the life and practice of many Christian churches. One or more days of prayer for Christian unity are usually celebrated near the liturgical commemoration of the conversion of Saint Paul, toward the end of each January, or around the time of Pentecost. The author speaks about his own powerful prayer experiences during meetings with representatives of various Christian communities in the following words:

> With profound emotion I remember praying together with the Primate of the Anglican Communion at Canterbury Cathedral (29 May 1982); in that magnificent edifice, I saw "an eloquent witness both to our long years of common inheritance and to the sad years of division that followed." Nor can I forget the meetings held in the Scandinavian and Nordic Countries (1–10 June 1989), in North and South America and in Africa, and at the headquarters of the World Council of Churches (12 June 1984), the organization committed to calling its member Churches and Ecclesial Communities "to

the goal of visible unity in one faith and in one Eucharistic fellowship expressed in worship and in common life in Christ." And how could I ever forget taking part in the Eucharistic Liturgy in the Church of Saint George at the Ecumenical Patriarchate (30 November 1979), and the service held in Saint Peter's Basilica during the visit to Rome of my Venerable Brother, Patriarch Dimitrios I (6 December 1987). . . . It is hard to describe in a few words the unique nature of each of these occasions of prayer. (*UUS* 24)

The Holy Father often refers to the teaching of the Second Vatican Council when dealing with themes of ecumenism or the meaning of prayer. Writing about prayer, he reminds us of the idea of spiritual ecumenism as discussed during the Second Vatican Council. To its essence belong conversion of the heart on one hand, and personal holiness combined with prayers for unity among all Christians on the other. The prayers of various ecclesial communities contribute to the mutual reconciliation even when the nature and goals of these prayers are not properly ecumenical. The achievement and maintenance of peace in the world are among such important goals of prayer.

John Paul II reminds us also that everybody not merely can but most definitely should contribute daily to the achievement of desired unity among Christians by means of their prayers, so that "there will be one flock, one shepherd" (Jn 10:16) as soon as possible. The Pope expresses this thought very forcefully: "Praying for unity is not a matter reserved only to those who actually experience the lack of unity among Christians. In the deep personal dialogue which each of us must carry on with the Lord in prayer, concern for unity cannot be absent" (*UUS* 27).

13 Faith and Reason
(*Fides et Ratio*)

September 14, 1998

Introduction

P EOPLE, AS LONG as they are aware of their existence, search for the truth about themselves, God, and the world around them. When we deal with the issue of the search for truth, we might well recall Pilate's question during the trial of Jesus: "What is truth?" (Jn 18:38).

Aristotle, a great ancient philosopher, defined truth as "a consonance between intellect and objective reality" (*FR* 56). What is also very important to realize is the fact that the human mind has the desire to discover truth. The science that deals with the issues of rational knowledge and search for truth is called philosophy. Theology, on the other hand, is the science that investigates and contemplates the truth as revealed by God. Other disciplines of science, such as informatics, cybernetics, or those branches of human knowledge that deal with technical discoveries are neutral with respect to the truth because they do not search for the answers to human existential questions and desires.

In his thirteenth encyclical, entitled *Fides et Ratio* (*Faith and Reason*), Pope John Paul II demonstrates the complementarity or connectivity of the two branches of the science of truth: philosophy and theology. A human being, while getting to know the world by means of reason, slowly but surely reaches the point of discovering the truth revealed by God. Faith, on the other hand, as God's gift, enriches the potentialities and directs the abilities of the human mind toward the discovery of this truth. In the very first sentence of his encyclical, the author affirms that "faith and reason are like two wings on which the human spirit rises to the contemplation of truth" (*FR* 1).

The Holy Father proclaimed the current encyclical on the twentieth anniversary of his pontificate and directed it to the bishops of the Catholic Church. The significance and the high status of philosophical studies in theological seminaries is one of the key issues dealt with in the document. Bishops have the responsibility for the level of these studies in their dioceses. John Paul II conducts a deep analysis of contemporary culture while referring to the relationships between faith and reason and between philosophy and theology. He points to the dangers facing the faith from some worldviews and ideologies hostile to Christianity, just as Leo XIII did in his Encyclical *Aeterni Patris* in 1879. In the second half of the nineteenth century, Leo XIII cautioned the faithful against positivistic thinking expressed in uncritical scientism and moral relativism. Scientism, namely, brands everything that has to do with the meaning of life as irrational. At the end of the twentieth century, John Paul II bemoans the tragedy of the separation between faith and reason. One of the consequences of this separation is the subjective understanding of truth: some believe in their version of truth regardless of objective truth.

John Paul II mentions the crisis of philosophy in the face of spreading relativism, a trend of thought that holds that objective truth does not exist, and therefore its discovery is impossible. People who accept such a premise live in the delusion of nihilism, that is, with a sense of hopelessness and despair. As the author cogently states: "Our age has been termed by some thinkers the age of 'postmodernity.' . . . The currents of thought which claim to be postmodern merit appropriate attention. According to some of them, the time of certainties is irrevocably past, and the human being must now learn to live in a horizon of total absence of meaning, where everything is provisional and ephemeral" (*FR* 91).

According to the Pope, the cure for those left in despair by nihilism and lost as the result of relativism can come from the reconstruction of the "sapiential" dimension of thinking, the type of thinking that asks primarily about the meaning of life. He makes us aware that uncertainty will never make us happy because to be human means to be a seeker, to be "*the one who seeks the truth*" (*FR* 28).

"Know Yourself"

The author entitled the introduction to his encyclical with the words of the admonition that used to be carved on the temple portal at Delhi: "Know yourself." He demonstrates in his encyclical that the knowledge of self is related to the discovery of answers to such existential questions as "*Who am I? Where have I come from and where am I going? Why is there evil? What is there after this life?*" (*FR* 1). The answer to the question "Who am I?" is simple enough: I am a *human being*! The Second Vatican Council paid much attention to the human person, and the Holy Father John Paul II himself placed the person at the center of his teaching. In the current document, he strives to make people aware of the possibility of knowing themselves by means of both faith and reason. He believes that only as the result of such knowledge can people grasp all the dimensions of their moral choices and assume full responsibility for their deeds. Only consistent and determined search for truth can lead people to Christ, who said about himself: "I am the way and the truth and the life" (Jn 14:6). This is the reason why John Paul II, right from the beginning of his pontificate, proclaimed with utter conviction the truth that people cannot know themselves profoundly and completely without Christ.

The Pope tells us in his work that two sciences, philosophy and theology, help people in their search for truth and for the meaning of life. He is, however, opposed to some contemporary ideological tendencies that deny philosophy's claim to be an authentic science, even though it was the first to emerge as such in ancient Greece. This is the reason why he believes that all philosophers should be marked by the comprehensive and passionate love for wisdom in every aspect of their activity: both when they fathom the depths of existential questions, and when they convey their reflections to others. Only under these conditions can philosophy help people truly know themselves. Otherwise, people run the risk of being deceived or manipulated by this most ancient of sciences.

John Paul II speaks in the following way about human desires to know the ultimate truth of existence, the key to self-knowledge: "Driven by the desire to discover the ultimate truth of existence, human beings seek to acquire those universal elements of knowledge which enable them to understand themselves better and to advance in their own self-realization. These fundamental elements of knowledge spring from the *wonder* awakened in them by the contemplation of creation. . . . Without wonder, men and women would lapse into deadening routine and little by little would become incapable of a life which is genuinely personal" (*FR* 4). The above quotation clearly demonstrates that people need to know themselves not only by means of faith, that is, by their obedience to revealed truth, but also with the help of reason, that is, on the basis of the wisdom of philosophy. In their efforts to know themselves, by means of faith and by means of reason, people search for truth so as to be free. This is exactly what Christ said: "You will know the truth, and the truth will set you free" (Jn 8:32).

The Holy Father deals with another dangerous phenomenon in contemporary culture, namely, a widely held opinion that human reason is not capable of discovering the truth. He remarks that with a similar premise, and with the simultaneous removal of metaphysics from philosophy, that is, with the intentional diversion of attention from higher realities of human existence and from God, "everything is reduced to opinion" (*FR* 5).

Mutual Dependence of Faith and Reason

The metaphor of the two wings the author used at the beginning of the encyclical shows the need for mutual dependence of faith and reason. If faith were to try to venture to the sky alone without reason, it would be doomed to an inevitable fall. The same may be said about reason deprived of the support of faith. Therefore, both faith and reason are the ways toward truth, the truth that human beings have not created. We have a natural capacity to know the world, self, and God by means of our reason and higher emotions. But we simply believe in the truths revealed by God. The Pope reminds us that every person's life, right from the day of birth, is full of various traditions and rituals that convey not only a certain language and culture but also the important truths that people later believe as if naturally. These truths can be challenged, critically evaluated, and subsequently accepted again if during the process of maturation, people verify them with their reason. John Paul II observes that

> there are in the life of a human being many more truths which are simply believed than truths which are acquired by way of personal verification. Who, for instance, could assess critically the countless scientific findings upon which modern life is based? Who could personally examine the flow of information which comes day after day from all parts of the world and

which is generally accepted as true? Who in the end could forge anew the paths of experience and thought which have yielded the treasures of human wisdom and religion? This means that the human being—the one who seeks the truth—is also *the one who lives by belief* (*FR* 31).

The Holy Father draws our attention to the fact that there are very many ways that people might take in their search for truth. Among the many possibilities he considers to be the best are those types of philosophy that directly formulate questions about the meaning of life and actively engage in the search for the answers to them. He states that "philosophy emerges . . . as one of noblest of human tasks. According to its Greek etymology, the term philosophy means 'love of wisdom'" (*FR* 3). We discover in the following sentences of the encyclical that the desire to discover truth is an essential element of human nature. Similar reciprocal influence occurs in theology as well as philosophy, especially if we continue the traditions of various philosophical and theological schools elaborated throughout the centuries.

Speaking about the methodologies of theology and philosophy—two distinct but interacting disciplines of science, the Pope draws our attention to the fact that

> theology makes its own the content of Revelation as this has been gradually expounded in Sacred Tradition, Sacred Scripture and the Church's living Magisterium (see *Dei Verbum* 10). . . . Philosophy contributes specifically to theology in preparing for a correct *auditus fidei* with its study of the structure of knowledge and personal communication, especially the various forms and functions of language. No less important is philosophy's contribution to a more coherent understanding of Church Tradition, the pronouncements of the Magisterium and the teaching of the great masters of theology, who often adopt concepts and thought-forms drawn from a particular philosophical tradition . . . in order to formulate correct and consistent interpretations (*FR* 65).

The pages of *Fides et Ratio* convey a clear message. The Pope addresses all who search for the truth in the words of Saint Paul: "*You are no longer strangers and sojourners, but you are saints and members of the household of God*" (Eph 2:19, in *FR* 70).

Antagonism between Faith and Reason

The content of the Encyclical *Fides et Ratio* offers contemporary humanity the hope of finding answers to the existential problems with which it wrestles, contrary to the widespread opinion that faith and reason have nothing in common. The Pope is aware of the fact that some people today do not believe in the existence of God and base their views of a human being on a false foundation. They do not recognize the role of reason in the human desire to discover metaphysical truth. Those who inherit this type of thinking, typical of the Enlightenment and stained by positivism about the self-sufficiency of the world, reject Christianity because it allegedly does not fulfill the needs of contemporary humanity.

John Paul II includes the following trends of thought among those that distort harmony between faith and reason: eclecticism, historicism, scientism, pragmatism, postmodernism, and nihilism. He devotes a few words of explanation to each.

Eclecticism

This denotes an attitude of those who, in their search for truth and in their way of constructing arguments and theological premises, "tend to use individual ideas drawn from different philosophies, without concern for their internal coherence, their place within a system or their historical context." The Pope states that in this way they "run the risk of being unable to distinguish the part of truth of a given doctrine from elements of it which may be erroneous or ill-suited to the task at hand. An extreme form of eclecticism appears also in the rhetorical misuse of philosophical terms to which some theologians are given at times. Such manipulation does not help the search for truth and does not train reason . . . to formulate arguments seriously and scientifically" (*FR* 86).

Historicism

The Holy Father sees the most characteristic feature of historicism in the choice of a certain philosophy as true on the basis of this philosophy's compliance with the demands of a given epoch and its ability to fulfill a set of given historical tasks. He observes: "At least implicitly . . . the enduring validity of truth is denied. What was true in one period, historicists claim, may not be true in another" (*FR* 87).

Scientism

A philosophical conception that does not recognize the value of any other forms of knowledge other than those proper to physical sciences, scientism thus reduces the value of religious and theological knowledge to that of a mere creation of our imagination and rejects the whole field of ethical knowledge as well. The author of the encyclical explains that "scientism consigns all that has to do with the question of the meaning of life to the realm of the irrational or imaginary" (*FR* 88).

Pragmatism

This way of thinking belongs to those who make moral choices without referring to ethical values or principles. John Paul II says that this trend of thinking has important practical consequences, as it has contributed to the "growing support for a concept of democracy which is not grounded upon any reference to unchanging values: whether or not a line of action is admissible is decided by the vote of a parliamentary majority (cf. *Evangelium Vitae* 69)" (*FR* 89).

Postmodernism

This trend undermines everything that is unchangeable.

Nihilism

This stems to some extent from the tragic experiences that plagued the twentieth century. In the face of the tragedy of these experiences, "rationalist optimism, which viewed history as the triumphant progress of reason, the source of all happiness and freedom" has collapsed. As a result, the Pope remarks, "one of our greatest threats is the temptation to despair" (*FR* 91).

Timeliness of Saint Thomas Aquinas's Ideas

Saint Thomas Aquinas loved truth. This is the reason why he is the model to be imitated by all those who search for truth, as the author of the encyclical affirms. The Pope points out that in the thought of this great medieval theologian and philosopher "the demands of reason and the power of faith found the most elevated synthesis ever attained by human thought, for he could defend the radical newness introduced by Revelation without ever demeaning the venture proper to reason" (*FR* 78).

The wisdom of Saint Thomas and the loftiness of his thought have retained their value today because nobody has matched his logical explanations of all the mysteries of God (see *Summa theologiae*) or his profound presentation of the important issues related to human life. Each one of us can find in his philosophy and theology the source of inspiration regarding one's vocation, destiny, development, and other areas of life. Saint Thomas possessed an exceptional ability of giving pertinent answers to the existential questions of people. His entire work has been compared to the gothic cathedrals that were built in his days.

John Paul II quotes a passage written by his predecessor, Pope Paul VI, on the seventh centenary of the death of the Angelic Doctor, as Saint Thomas is also called:

> Without doubt, Thomas possessed supremely the courage of the truth, a freedom of spirit in confronting new problems, the intellectual honesty of those who allow Christianity to be contaminated neither by secular philosophy nor by a prejudiced rejection of it. He passed therefore into the history of Christian thought as a pioneer of the new path of philosophy and universal culture. The key point and almost the kernel of the solution which, with all the brilliance of his prophetic intuition, he gave to the new encounter of faith and reason was a reconciliation between the secularity of the world and the radicality of the Gospel, thus avoiding the unnatural tendency to negate the world and its values while at the same time keeping faith with the supreme and inexorable demands of the supernatural order. (Apostolic Letter *Lumen Ecclesiae* 8, in *FR* 43)

What is exceptional in the wisdom of Saint Thomas is his firm conviction about the importance of the supernatural power of faith without forgetting the value of reason. We learn from this great theologian that faith is a grace, that is, a gift of God, and although God always gives us a chance to deepen our faith (see 1 Cor 3:6), it is by means of our reason that we can make it happen if we respond to the divine initiative wholeheartedly. Human wisdom, according to Saint Thomas, is the most specific feature that has been inscribed somewhere within us, and it reaches our consciousness through the working of the Holy Spirit and through the voice of our conscience.

The Holy Father expresses his thoughts about wisdom:

Another of the great insights of Saint Thomas was his perception of the role of the Holy Spirit in the process by which knowledge matures into wisdom. From the first pages of his *Summa Theologiae*, Aquinas was keen to show the primacy of the wisdom which is the gift of the Holy Spirit and which opens the way to a knowledge of divine realities. . . . "The wisdom named among the gifts of the Holy Spirit is distinct from the wisdom found among the intellectual virtues. This second wisdom is acquired through study, but the first 'comes from on high' (*Summa Theologiae* II–II, 45, 1 ad 2). . . . Yet the priority accorded this wisdom does not lead the Angelic Doctor to overlook the presence of two other complementary forms of wisdom—*philosophical* wisdom, which is based upon the capacity of the intellect, . . . and *theological* wisdom, which is based upon Revelation and which explores the contents of faith, entering the very mystery of God. (*FR* 44)

Fathers of the Church on the Relation between Faith and Reason

All the ideas of John Paul II recorded in the Encyclical *Fides et Ratio* point to the greatness of human potential to know self and God by means of faith and reason. In order to show the complementarity of faith and reason from a historical perspective, the Pope presents the opinions of some great thinkers of the past and selected Fathers of the Church. He reminds us that already in the Acts of the Apostles the Christian message had to confront the philosophy contemporary to the time. A dispute of Saint Paul with "some of the Epicurean and Stoic philosophers" (Acts 17:18) in Athens is a good example of this process. The Holy Father stresses that "if pagans were to understand them, the first Christians could not refer only to 'Moses and the prophets' when they spoke. They had to point as well to natural knowledge of God and to the voice of conscience in every human being" (*FR* 36).

In a subsequent section of his encyclical, the author reminds us that the relationship between Christianity and philosophy was not always a cozy one. Fortunately, humanity understood with the passage of time that the knowledge of philosophy makes the understanding of faith easier, especially in view of the fact that one of the new ideas brought by Christianity was "the affirmation of the right of everyone to have access to the truth" (*FR* 38).

The Pope includes Saint Justin and Origen among the pioneers of a constructive dialogue between the early Christianity and philosophy. The latter of the two thinkers, "assuming many elements of Platonic thought, . . . begins to construct an early form of Christian theology" (*FR* 39). The author of the encyclical emphasizes that Saint Augustine played a particularly important role in the process of Christianizing Platonic and neo-Platonic thought by creating the first great synthesis of philosophical and theological ideas. The Augustinian system was known and used in the West for centuries. As we move ahead with our survey of philosophy in history, we cannot fail to notice that in Scholastic theology the role of reason in philosophy becomes ever more crucial. According to Saint Anselm, the holy Archbishop of Canterbury in the eleventh century and one of the founders of Scholasticism, "the priority of faith is not in competition with the search which is proper to reason" (*FR* 42).

The Holy Father underlines that in the development process being described here Saint Thomas Aquinas played a crucial role, "because of the dialogue which he undertook with the Arab and Jewish thought of his time. In an age when Christian thinkers were rediscovering the treasures of ancient philosophy, and more particularly of Aristotle, Thomas had the great merit of giving pride of place to the harmony which exists between faith and reason. Both the light of reason and the light of faith come from God, he argued; hence there can be no contradiction between them" (*FR* 43).

John Paul II reminds us the two arguably greatest representatives of Scholasticism, Saint Albert the Great and Saint Thomas, even though they upheld the interdependence of theology and philosophy, were the first to concede autonomy to other disciplines of science "if they were to perform well in their respective fields of research" (*FR* 45). Unfortunately, the exaggerated separation of theology from the remaining sciences and the subsequent emergence of rationalism brought about the appearance of certain philosophical trends that deprived faith of any rational foundations or justifications. Blindly following the unfolding cultural transformations, some philosophers abandoned the dignity of reason, which, in their view, was "no longer equipped to know the truth and to seek the absolute" (*FR* 47).

"Sapiential" Dimension of Philosophy

Apart from describing in his encyclical the logical link between faith and reason, and between philosophy and theology, the author draws our attention to the so-called eternal truths with which philosophy constantly grapples. We need divine wisdom to discover these truths. God himself allows us to know him in a similar fashion, through wisdom. John Paul II refers to the revealing words of Saint Paul (Eph 1:9), as paraphrased in the Vatican Council II Constitution *Dei Verbum* (2): "In his goodness and wisdom, God chose to reveal himself and to make known to us the hidden purpose of his will" (*FR* 7).

While describing the significance of philosophical thinking, the Pope does not refer merely to a university-based activity of a selected few. Instead, he directs the following words to everybody: "The truths of philosophy, it should be said, are not restricted only to the sometimes ephemeral teachings of professional philosophers. All men and women, as I have noted, are in some sense philosophers and have their own philosophical conceptions with which they direct their lives" (*FR* 30).

In this way, the Holy Father encourages everybody, including professional philosophers, to the contemplation of the Bible: "Sacred Scripture indicates with remarkably clear cues how deeply related are the knowledge conferred by faith and the knowledge conferred by reason; and it is *in the Wisdom literature* that this relationship is addressed most explicitly. What is striking about these biblical texts, if they are read without prejudice, is that they embody not only the faith of Israel, but also the treasury of cultures and civilizations which have long vanished" (*FR* 16).

The issue of trust is an important element of papal teaching, especially in the context of the "sapiential" dimension of knowledge. The author expresses his ideas in the following words: "Men and women are on a journey of discovery which is humanly unstoppable—a search for the truth and a search for a person to whom they might entrust themselves" (*FR* 33). It is natural that people, seeing the variability and fragility of everything that is human, desire to trust God. This is the reason why the Pope reminds us: "Christian faith comes to meet them [that is, people in search of truth], offering the concrete possibility of reaching the goal which they seek. Moving beyond the stage of simple believing, Christian faith immerses human beings in the order of grace, which enables them to share in the mystery of Christ, which in turn offers them a true and coherent knowledge of the Triune God. In Jesus Christ, who is the Truth, faith recognizes the ultimate appeal to humanity, an appeal made in order that what we experience as desire and nostalgia may come to its fulfillment" (*FR* 33).

The "sapiential" dimension of philosophy can find its expression in our admiration of the laws of nature and of the beauty of the world. John Paul

II reminds us of a thesis of Greek philosophy, also included in the Scriptures, which says that "in reasoning about nature, the human being can rise to God: 'From the greatness and beauty of created things comes a corresponding perception of their Creator' (Wis 13:5)" (*FR* 19).

Fides et Ratio is the author's call for true wisdom on the one hand, and for understanding the links between human knowledge and divine wisdom on the other. The encyclical is also a call for a symbiosis and an alliance between philosophy and theology in every individual's search for truth. The Holy Father expresses his ardent desire for Mary powerfully to intercede on behalf of all who look for divine truth and wisdom: "May Mary, Seat of Wisdom, be a sure haven for all who devote their lives to the search for wisdom. May their journey into wisdom, sure and final goal of all true knowing, be freed of every hindrance by the intercession of the one who, in giving birth to the Truth and treasuring it in her heart, has shared it forever with all the world" (*FR* 108).

14

The Church of the Eucharist
(*Ecclesia de Eucharistia*)

April 17, 2003

Introduction

THE PRINCIPAL SUBJECT of Pope John Paul II's fourteenth and final encyclical is the Eucharist. *Ecclesia de Eucharistia* (*The Church of the Eucharist*) was appropriately promulgated on Holy Thursday, April 17, 2003. In this document, he analyzes one of the greatest mysteries of our faith—the sacramental presence of God under the species of bread and wine. At the very beginning, the author draws our attention to the essential feature of the Eucharist, that is, the fact that it is the fruit of Jesus' death on the Cross, demonstrating in this way the close relationship between the Upper Room and the Cross. Referring back to his first encyclical about Christ as the Redeemer of Man, the Pope highlights its thematic connection to the present document, which deals with the Eucharist. Here he treats the most important issues related to the Eucharist in six chapters. He considers the Eucharist as a mystery of faith in the first chapter. In subsequent sections, he stresses the fact that the Eucharist contributes to the building of the Church, its apostolic character, and creation of ecclesial communion. Finally, he concludes his encyclical with the final two sections describing the beauty of the Eucharistic celebration and the Eucharistic faith of Mary.

The Holy Father is aware that in discussing the Eucharist, it is not sufficient to recite a formula out of a catechism, nor answer a simple question, such as "What is the Eucharist?" It is not proper, either, to present the interpretation of the Eucharist in terms of Sunday duty or liturgical celebration. This is the reason why he draws our attention to the fact that the Eucharist is a gift of God and must be experienced with our whole heart and full awareness of its grandeur. It is an ineffable mystery, and therefore the adoration of Jesus in the Most Blessed Sacrament cannot be expressed with mere words. The Pope's deep absorption during the celebration of the Eucharist, of this the greatest of sacraments, indicates his awareness of this mystery, and his profound respect for Jesus' words during the Last Supper: "Drink from it, all of you, for this is my blood of the covenant, which will be shed on behalf of many for the forgiveness of sins" (Mt 26:27–28). "This is my blood of the covenant, which will be shed for many" (see Mk 14:24; see also Lk 22:20; 1 Cor 11:25). The adoration of the Eucharist changes naturally into thanksgiving. This is, in fact, the original meaning of word *eucharist*—"thanksgiving." It is gratitude for the immense love of God who gave us his own Son—so that he could die for our sins and remain with us sacramentally until the end of time. The Holy Mass thus demonstrates the sacrifice of the Cross, because the Eucharist is bound with the offering of Jesus' life. The Savior himself speaks about it in the following words: "No one has greater love than this, to lay down one's life for one's friends" (Jn 15:13).

Apart from the adoration of the Eucharist and thanksgiving for this great gift, John Paul II speaks about the emotion that should be experienced at such a great mystery: "This amazement should always fill the Church assembled for the celebration of the Eucharist" (*EdeE* 5). He recalls many places in different corners of the world where he celebrated the Eucharist over the years and speaks about its cosmic dimension. He reminds us at this point that even when the Eucharist "is celebrated on the humble altar of a country church, the Eucharist is always in some way celebrated *on the altar of the world*. It unites heaven and earth. It embraces and permeates all creation" (*EdeE* 8).

Eucharist Builds the Church

The Pope begins his encyclical with the statement "the Church draws her life from the Eucharist" (*EdeE* 1). Along the course of history, from the time of the Upper Room until today, many people have drawn spiritual power from the Eucharist, even without being able to express the nature of this amazing sacrament, which involves a tremendous mystery of our faith. Expressing the Church's continuous care for the Eucharist, the Pope reminds us of a number of recent important documents devoted to this mystery:

> In times closer to our own, three Encyclical Letters should be mentioned: *Mirae Caritatis* of Leo XIII (28 May 1902); *Mediator Dei* of Pius XII (20 November 1947); and *Mysterium Fidei* of Paul VI (3 September 1965). . . . I myself, in the first years of my apostolic ministry in the Chair of Peter, wrote the Apostolic Letter *Dominicae Cenae* (24 February 1980), in which I discussed some aspects of the Eucharistic mystery. . . . Today I take up anew the thread of that argument, with even greater emotion and gratitude in my heart, echoing as it were the word of the Psalmist: "What shall I render to the Lord for all his bounty to me? I will lift up the cup of salvation and call on the name of the Lord (Ps 116:12–13)." (*EdeE* 9)

As in his prior encyclicals, John Paul II repeatedly refers to the teachings of the Second Vatican Council. Underlining the role of the Eucharist in the life of the Church, he quotes the Vatican Council II Dogmatic Constitution *Lumen Gentium* (11), and concludes that the Eucharistic sacrifice is "the source and summit of the Christian life" (*EdeE* 1).

Each year the Pope discussed various aspects of the Eucharist in his letters directed to all priests, and through them, to all the faithful of the Church. The Year of the Eucharist, which he proclaimed and which lasted from October 2004 to October 2005, was another opportunity for the faithful to meditate on the Eucharistic mystery.

When Pope John Paul II speaks about the Eucharist building the Church, he has in mind the whole Church, that is, ordained ministers, consecrated people who are members of religious orders, and the laity. While celebrating or participating in Holy Mass, each one of us should draw from the Eucharistic Christ the spiritual strength so as to properly fulfill the duties of life and transform the world, utilizing the spirit of gospel values. Therefore, the Holy Father speaks about the Eucharist as the mystery of faith, and at the same time the mystery of light. He emphasizes that every time the Eucharistic sacrifice is celebrated, "the faithful can in some way relive the experience of the two disciples on the road to Emmaus: 'their eyes were opened and they recognized him' (Lk 24:31)" (*EdeE* 6). The faithful need the light of faith in order to recognize Christ present in the Eucharist under the species of bread and wine, to lead an ethical life, and to create bonds with others, at home and in society, that are based on love. This is the reason why, as the author points out, the Eucharist, while contributing to the building of the Church, "creates human community" (*EdeE* 24).

The Holy Mass as Sacrifice is excellence in itself as well as a creator of unity among peoples. Both of these facets are extremely important ways in which the Eucharist supports the Church. The Pope employs an image used by Saint John Chrysostom to illustrate the truth of the essential unity of all who participate in the Eucharist: "For what is the bread? It is the body of Christ. . . . For as bread is completely one, though made of up many grains of wheat, and these, albeit unseen, remain nonetheless present, in such a way that their difference is not apparent since they have been made a perfect whole, so too are we mutually joined to one another and together united with Christ" (*In Epistolam I ad Corinthios Homiliae*, 24, 2: PG 61, 200; in *EdeE* 23).

The Apostolic Character of the Eucharist

The Eucharist was instituted by Christ himself. The Holy Father John Paul II explains that Jesus entrusted it to us through the mediation of the apostles and their successors. He reminds us that the Eucharist builds the Church, while the Church celebrates the Eucharist. Thus we have a two-way relationship. The Pope underlines that this truth allows us to "apply to the Eucharistic mystery the very words with which, in the Nicene-Constantinopolitan Creed, we profess the Church to be 'one, holy, catholic and apostolic.' The Eucharist too is one and catholic" (*EdeE* 26).

In order to better understand the issue at stake, the Pope reminds us that the Church is apostolic, because Jesus himself chose the twelve apostles on whose foundation he built her (see Eph 2:20). The apostles are also at the foundation of the Eucharist, because the Church celebrating the Eucharist across the centuries continually maintains the activity of the apostles "in obedience to the Lord's command" (*EdeE* 27).

Contrary to some contemporary liberal tendencies, which attempt to eliminate the sacrificial dimension of the Holy Mass and to separate the Eucharist from the sacramental priesthood, Pope John Paul II teaches that only a validly ordained priest has the right to celebrate the Eucharist. He clearly differentiates the role of the laity from that of a priest during the Eucharist. He appeals to the documents of the Second Vatican Council, and teaches that "'the faithful join in the offering of the Eucharist by virtue of their royal priesthood', yet it is the ordained priest who, 'acting in the person of Christ, brings about the Eucharistic Sacrifice and offers it to God in the name of all the people'. For this reason, the Roman Missal prescribes that only the priest should recite the Eucharistic Prayer, while the people participate in faith and in silence" (*EdeE* 28).

The Holy Father stresses that the priest who celebrates the Eucharistic sacrifice acts *in persona Christi*, which means much more than just in the name of, or in place of Christ:"

> "*In persona* means in specific sacramental identification with the eternal High Priest who is the author and principal subject of this sacrifice of his, a sacrifice in which, in truth, nobody can take his place" (Apostolic Letter *Dominicae Cenae*) The ministry of priests who have received the sacrament of Holy Orders, in the economy of salvation chosen by Christ, makes clear that the Eucharist which they celebrate is *a gift which radically transcends the power of the assembly* and is in any event essential for validly linking the Eucharistic consecration to the sacrifice of the Cross and to the Last Supper. (*EdeE* 29)

Just as the author did in his Encyclical *Ut Unum Sint*, so also in the presently described one about the Eucharist, he expresses his great desire for Christian unity, but not at the expense of distorting the truth of Christ. The Holy Mass, namely, is not the property of a priest, a bishop, nor a pope, and therefore nobody is allowed to change on his or her own accord the will of Christ in relation to the individual sacraments. The Pope teaches this truth in the following words:

> The Catholic faithful, therefore, while respecting the religious convictions of these separated brethren, must refrain from receiving the communion distributed in their celebrations, so as not to condone an ambiguity about the nature of the Eucharist and, consequently, to fail in their duty to bear clear witness to the truth. This would result in slowing the progress being made towards full visible unity. Similarly, it is unthinkable to substitute for Sunday Mass ecumenical celebrations of the word or services of common prayer with Christians from the aforementioned Ecclesial Communities. . . .

The fact that the power of consecrating the Eucharist has been entrusted only to Bishops and priests does not represent any kind of belittlement of the rest of the People of God, for in the communion of the one body of Christ which is the Church this gift redounds to the benefit of all. (*EdeE* 30)

Eucharist and Ecclesial Communion

John Paul II teaches us in his encyclical that the Eucharist, thanks to which we achieve perfect communion with the invisible God, unites the faithful in a visible manner through the mediation of the priest who celebrates the Eucharistic sacrifice. He stresses the importance of the relationship between the two dimensions of communion, as follows: "The profound relationship between the invisible and the visible elements of ecclesial communion is constitutive of the Church as the sacrament of salvation" (*EdeE* 35).

What determines the depth of our communion with God is the practice of faith, hope, and love, as well as life in the state of sanctifying grace, by which we "come to share in the divine nature" (2 Pet 1:4). The preservation of these invisible links is an indispensable duty of a Christian who desires to participate fully in the Eucharist by receiving the Body and Blood of Christ. The author, however, reminds and warns us in the words of Saint John Chrysostom that " 'no one [should] draw near to this sacred table with a sullied and corrupt conscience. Such an act, in fact, can never be called 'communion', not even were we to touch the Lord's body a thousand times over, but 'condemnation', 'torment' and 'increase of punishment'. Along these same lines, the *Catechism of the Catholic Church* rightly stipulates that 'anyone conscious of a grave sin must receive the sacrament of Reconciliation before coming to communion' " (*EdeE* 36).

We see then that the sacraments of the Eucharist and Reconciliation are closely related. If the Eucharist makes present the salvific sacrifice of the Cross in a sacramental way, as the Pope instructs us, it also necessitates our constant conversion, in view of the words that Saint Paul directed to the Christians in Corinth: "We beseech you on behalf of Christ, be reconciled to God" (2 Cor 5:20, in *EdeE* 37).

Speaking about the visible aspect of the communion created by the Eucharist, the Pope draws our attention to the parish, where priests bear moral responsibility for the observance of the principles communicated by

Christ to be cultivated in his Church. The sacrament of Baptism constitutes the visible foundation of this ecclesial communion. Saint Paul spoke
about it in the following words: "For in one Spirit we were all baptized into
one body" (1 Cor 12:13). Similarly, John Paul II points out: "It is not possible to give communion to a person who is not baptized or to one who
rejects the full truth of the faith regarding the Eucharistic mystery. Christ is
the truth and he bears witness to the truth (cf. Jn 14:6; 18:37); the sacrament of his body and blood does not permit duplicity" (*EdeE* 38).

The author also tells us that the ecclesial communion of any Eucharistic
assembly is a communion with one's proper bishop and with the pope. He
therefore writes that "the Bishop, in effect, is the *visible* principle and the
foundation of unity within his particular Church (*Lumen Gentium* 23). It
would therefore be a great contradiction if the sacrament . . . of the Church's
unity were celebrated without true communion with the Bishop. . . . 'Every
valid celebration of the Eucharist expresses this universal communion with
Peter and with the whole Church, or objectively calls for it, as in the case of
the Christian Churches separated from Rome' (Letter *Communionis Notio*)"
(*EdeE* 39).

Referring to ecumenical efforts, the Holy Father reminds us: "While it
is never legitimate to concelebrate in the absence of full communion, the
same is not true with respect to the administration of the Eucharist *under
special circumstances, to individual persons* belonging to Churches or Ecclesial Communities not in full communion with the Catholic Church. In
this case, in fact, the intention is to meet a grave spiritual need . . . of an
individual believer, not to bring about an *intercommunion* which remains
impossible until the visible bonds of ecclesial communion are fully re-
established" (*EdeE* 45).

The Beauty of the Eucharistic Celebration

Many various forms enriching the celebration appeared during the history
of the Church out of respect for the Eucharist. Among them are beautiful
songs and melodies, including Gregorian chant, decorative golden chalices
and tabernacles, richly embroidered chasubles, sculptures, paintings, and
last but not least, imposing architecture, cathedrals, and basilicas. Are all
these manifestations of creative genius of pious people to be seen as mere
acts of waste, as Judas Iscariot thought on seeing Mary, Lazarus's sister,

pour on Jesus' feet a flask of precious ointment (see Jn 12:5)? Judas had his argument: he claimed that the money gained by selling the ointment could have been used financially to support many poor people. We cannot, however, impose limits on other people's generosity flowing from the need of their hearts.

The Pope thinks that the Eucharist shaped the Church, her spirituality, and "has also powerfully affected 'culture', and the arts in particular" (*EdeE* 49). He also states the fact that what took place in the areas of ecclesial art and liturgical discipline in ancient Christian territories happens on continents where Christianity is relatively young as well. This phenomenon is in accordance with the guidance of the Second Vatican Council, which speaks of "the need for sound and proper 'inculturation'" (*EdeE* 51). Aware of the need to express Eucharistic spirituality in the forms proper to every culture, on one hand, the author warns against distortions of the sacrament "through forms of experimentation or practices introduced without a careful review on the part of the competent ecclesiastical authorities" (*EdeE* 51), on the other.

Referring to the need for deep respect to the Eucharist, the Pope states that

> in the years following the post-conciliar liturgical reform, as a result of a misguided sense of creativity and adaptation there have been a number of *abuses* which have been a source of suffering for many. . . . I consider it my duty, therefore to appeal urgently that the liturgical norms for the celebration of the Eucharist be observed with great fidelity. These norms are a concrete expression of the authentically ecclesial nature of the Eucharist. . . . Liturgy is never anyone's private property, be it of the celebrant or of the community in which the mysteries are celebrated. (*EdeE* 52)

In the final part of his document, as in his earlier encyclicals, the Holy Father points to the faith of Mary. He again depicts her deep Eucharistic faith in the current encyclical. He reminds us of her telling encounter with Saint Elizabeth. At the time, Mary was already with child by the action of the Holy Spirit (see Lk 1:35) and became, as the author notes, "the first 'tabernacle' in history . . . in which the Son of God, still invisible to our human gaze, allowed himself to be adored by Elizabeth" (*EdeE* 55). The Pope underlines the fact that Mary is present during every Holy Mass. He asks an important question: Is she not an unsurpassable model of love and inspiration during every Eucharistic communion? Subsequently, John Paul II encourages us to get acquainted with the Eucharistic piety of great masters, and with that of the Mother of the Redeemer in particular. "Above all, let us *listen to Mary Most Holy*, in whom the mystery of the Eucharist appears . . . as a *mystery of light*. Gazing upon Mary, we come to know *the transforming power present in the Eucharist*. In her we see the world renewed in love" (*EdeE* 62).

15 Concluding Reflection

POPE JOHN PAUL II became the spiritual leader of millions of people in his time thanks to his closeness to God, which was reflected in his demeanor, his natural modesty that fascinated all those who had a chance to meet him, and the acquired wisdom which he shared with everyone who was ready to listen. One of the most important truths that he resolutely taught all along as priest, bishop, and pope was the sanctity of human life. He proclaimed with unshakable conviction that human life is God's gift. He repeatedly reminded us of the fifth commandment of the Decalogue, "Do not kill," because nobody has the right to terminate human life under any circumstance or pretext.

The Pope taught that God had granted us conscience (that is, the faculty to recognize a moral law) and freedom (that is, the ability to make morally significant choices). John Paul II pointed to the danger of distorting this precious gift of conscience by the uncritical acceptance of an ever-greater amount of available information. This situation necessitates the formation of our conscience in accordance with God's teaching as expressed in the Bible and the Magisterium of the Church. We should use our freedom judiciously and always relate it to the truth because only a freedom based on truth can save us from repeating the mistake of the first people deceived by Satan (see Gen 3:5). In the Encyclical *Veritatis Splendor*, the Pope stated that "man, by the use of reason, participates in the eternal law, which it is not for him to establish" (*VS* 36).

The Holy Father invited every person to strive to achieve internal integration, which consists in the formation of conscience according to the divine law and manifests itself in a life of loving service to others. Once we have fully assimilated God's values we are able to serve others in our families, in the places where we work, and in all circumstances of life.

If instead we reject the divine perspective on reality, we risk developing an attitude of striving to have more material things rather than of aspiring to be more of a human being. Greed, egocentrism, and distrust will replace our natural generosity, cultivated ability to focus on others, and childlike trust. This evolution would go contrary to the spiritual transformation that Jesus spoke about in his conversation with Nicodemus and that is nothing short of a new birth (see Jn 3:3). The possibility of a new life in Jesus is the Good News that Pope John Paul II proclaimed and desired so much to be made known to all the nations of the world thanks to renewed, enthusiastic, and methodical evangelization.

The Pope was convinced that people who have learned how to be truly human will become kind and sensitive to others, especially to the poor, and able to meet their needs. Mother Earth, rich as she is in natural resources, is able to feed all of God's children: it is the greed of some of these children that renders prosperity for everyone impossible. The gospel of love that Jesus proclaimed and John Paul II defended can change this unjust and unnatural situation. The contemporary world is characterized by an inequality and social injustice that only love has the power to supplant. The Pope diagnosed this dire state of humanity when he wrote: "The principal obstacle to be overcome on the way to authentic liberation is sin and the structures produced by sin as it multiplies and spreads.... 'For where truth and love are missing, the process of liberation results in the death of a freedom which will have lost all support.' (*Libertatis Conscientia* 24)" (*Sollicitudo Rei Socialis* 46).

When John Paul II returned to the Father's house, millions of people around the globe unanimously demanded that he be promptly proclaimed a saint. "Santo subito!" shouted the crowd gathered for the extraordinary funeral of the Pope in Saint Peter's Square in Rome. In view of the fact that he had been a spiritual leader and a moral authority for a huge part of humanity for a quarter of a century, this demand was fully justified.

John Paul II was an outstanding personality in more ways than one. We can understand him better when we become acquainted with his fascinating lifestyle. We grow to appreciate him even more when we delve into the world of his theological and philosophical treaties and literary creations. We draw on a tremendous spiritual wealth when we analyze his teaching expressed in a most original and personal manner in his fourteen encyclicals. If this book has succeeded in bringing the reader closer to this font of spiritual treasure that the papal reflections most definitely are, it has more than served its purpose.

Index